More Morton
Greats

More Morton Greats

Graeme Ross

breedon **books**

PUBLISHING

First published in Great Britain in 2005 by
The Breedon Books Publishing Company Limited
Breedon House, 3 The Parker Centre,
Derby, DE21 4SZ.

I would like to dedicate this book to my father-in-law
'Teddy' and Ian Shearer.

ISBN 1 85983471 X

Printed and bound by Biddles, King's Lynn, Norfolk.

Contents

Acknowledgements

Just as with the original *Morton Greats* there are many people to thank. First of all, thanks to Breedon Books for their support. The subjects themselves were obviously a great help and very giving with their time and effort. Jim Bolster was very helpful with the chapter on his father-in-law Jimmy Gourlay. For photographs, again I have to thank the *Greenock Telegraph*, Grace Gough of *The Herald* and Danny Goodwin.

Others who were happy to help were Morton Football Club and Douglas Rae, Arthur Montford, Bob Crampsey, Mike Jackson, Hugh Strachan, Mark McGhee, Neil Orr, Jim Holmes, Roy Baines, Joe Jordan, Joe Harper, Jimmy Boyd, Allan McGraw, Lawrie Reilly, Sir Tom Finney, Richard McBrearty and Tommy Malcolm from the Scottish Football Museum, Bob Laird, David Sutherland, David Ross, author of *The Roar of the Crowd*, and Roger Graham and Chris Fitzgerald of the *Greenock Telegraph*.

The Watt Library in Greenock was an invaluable source of archive material, and the staff were an enormous help. Thanks to Keith Wilson of Smith's Sports Shop and Morton Unofficial.net for supporting *Morton Greats*. Special thanks to Morton's biggest fan, Pat Gillan. Remember the Dundee United game, Pat?

And finally, special thanks to my wife Ann and daughter Jennifer for their support, patience and understanding.

Apologies to anyone I have missed.

Introduction

Well here we go again. Another 10 Morton Greats. I had always felt that there was a market for a *Morton Greats* book, but even I was overwhelmed with the terrific response from Morton fans when the original *Morton Greats* was published. The memories of the signing sessions and the queue of Morton fans of all ages will live with me for a long time. So thanks to everyone who bought the original book, and were so complimentary about it.

As with the first book I have tried to cover different eras, and inevitably someone's favourite will again be missing. But hopefully there will be something in this book for everyone, and people will enjoy it as much as they seem to have enjoyed the original. It's been great fun writing these books, and of course one of the biggest thrills is actually meeting and talking with not just the subjects themselves, but legends of the game like Sir Tom Finney.

The book concludes not with a player, but a manager. The subtitle is 'The Best Ever?' Everyone will have their own opinion about whether Benny Rooney was the best ever Morton manager, but for a host of Morton fans, the Benny Rooney era was the most exciting in living memory and I think it's appropriate to conclude the book with Benny. And I think the book begins appropriately as well with a key figure in the club's greatest hour and a half, and indeed their history – Jimmy Gourlay. So here's to the 'Ton and promotion. 'Come on ye 'Ton!'

Foreword
by Douglas Rae

I feel honoured to have been asked by Graeme Ross to write the foreword for the second edition of his work, *Morton Greats*. It would be remiss of me not to thank Graeme for having found the time, the desire and the inspiration to compile this further record of Morton players who, over the past 80 years or so, have made a significant impact upon the history of our august club.

Like my great friend and fellow director, Arthur Montford, I have also supported Morton for over 60 years, in fact since I was nine years old. It was Arthur who took me to my first ever Morton match at Cappielow when Morton defeated Albion Rovers 5–1. With me it was love at first sight and since that first day my love and affection for Morton has never faltered or wavered.

Two matches played at Cappielow are amongst my early recollections; a Cup tie versus Clyde and the derby match against St Mirren on New Year's Day 1943. Both matches had the same outcome; 8–0 wins for Morton! Can you imagine the joy experienced in thrashing Saints 8–0? It really was little wonder that we won these two matches so decisively when one considers the players who graced our forward line on these two occasions. On the right wing we had English internationalist Stanley Matthews, who was possibly the greatest dribbler and ball crosser ever. At inside-right we had Jimmy Garth, who was a player of great skill, and at centre-forward we had another English international, Tommy Lawton, who bagged five goals against Clyde. Inside-left featured Billy Steel, who was a player of extraordinary talent and who commanded the record Scottish transfer when he was transferred from Morton to Derby for £15,500. Finally, on the left wing was Johnny 'Fingers' Kelly, who was a real old-fashioned winger who liked to beat his man, race to the corner flag and deliver crosses that were the envy of our opponents. These five players would have graced the finest team in Europe, yet for a period during the war they graced Morton; a forward line that left me with never-to-be-forgotten memories. Graeme will, I am sure, have unearthed many new facts for this book, which we will either have forgotten or have never known, so it is with great expectancy that I look forward to reading this new edition.

It is certainly not easy to write a book of this nature. It demands much time and patience in research and it is not an easy task deciding which players to include and which ones to leave out. In my view there have been many, many players whom one could describe as having been 'Morton Greats' and who have given enormous pleasure to our fans while bringing glory and focus to our club.

Thinking of 'Morton Greats', I believe that our loyal fans are certainly worthy of mention in that vein. What pleases me most about being a Morton supporter is that, irrespective of age or background, our love of Morton unites us all. Surely there is no other team like us?

Douglas Rae, Chairman, Morton Football Club
22 July 2005

Chapter 1

Jimmy Gourlay
The Original Mr Morton

For the casual football fan, the name Jimmy Gourlay is a mere footnote in the history of the Scottish game. For those who care about these things, Jimmy Gourlay's name appears in the records as the scorer of the only goal in the 1922 Scottish Cup Final. For most Morton fans, however, Jimmy Gourlay's name has gathered almost mythical status, and not just for that goal. Jimmy served Morton for over 40 years in many capacities. For many years he was the buffer between the management and the players. Jimmy attended to anything that needed to be done around the ground. Player, trainer, groundsman, confidante and friend to the players, and all who passed through Cappielow, there is a part of Morton Football Club that will forever be Jimmy Gourlay. His sphere of influence covered a 45-year period from before World War One to the late 1950s. When Jimmy was born, Charlie Chaplin and Adolf Hitler were not yet born, and Queen Victoria was still on the throne, yet he remains one of the key figures in Morton's history.

Jimmy Gourlay was born in the Ayrshire village of Annbank in 1888. He came from mining stock and was part of a large family, with six brothers who all played football in the Ayrshire Juniors. His father, known as 'White' Gourlay, was a keen footballer. 'White' won international caps at junior level and was a member of the Annbank side that won the first Qualifying Cup in 1895. On leaving school, Jimmy worked for a time down the pits along with most of his brothers, one of whom was killed in an accident in the pit. Jimmy's ambition was to be a professional footballer, however, and he played from an early age, eventually graduating to local junior side Annbank United. From Annbank, Jimmy took his first steps in the senior game when he moved to Port Glasgow Athletic, who were then a senior side in the Scottish First Division. The Scottish leagues at this time were full of sides long consigned to the history books. In 1908, when Jimmy signed for Port Glasgow, sides such as Leith Athletic and Abercorn from Paisley were features of the Scottish game. At this stage in his career Jimmy was an inside-forward and occasionally filled in at centre-forward.

Never the biggest of men at five feet seven, Jimmy made up for his lack of stature with his strong, powerful running, tenacious tackling and eye for a goal. The *Port Glasgow Express* of January 1909 observed that Gourlay was coming on in leaps and bounds: 'His speed is better and he is showing a confidence and command of the ball that makes his play most valuable.'

A particular feature of Jimmy's game was his powerful shooting, although the *Port Glasgow Express* football correspondent often criticised him for not shooting more often. The *Express* was indeed ahead of its time as it was also known to criticise referees, calling one unfortunate's performance in a Port Glasgow-Morton derby, 'exerable'. As fortune would have it, Jimmy had signed for Port Glasgow just as the club began a slide which would all too soon lead to their demise. For many years Port Glasgow were the pre-eminent side in the district and indeed Renfrewshire. Formed in 1881, Port Glasgow Athletic had won the Renfrewshire Cup five times and were founder members of the Scottish Second Division. As recently as 1906 they had contested the Scottish Cup semi-final, had a player capped by Scotland and had beaten Rangers at Clune Park. But they were now experiencing serious financial problems around the time of Jimmy's signing. By 1909 they were being forced to sell their best players. With the club entangled in a seemingly endless fight against relegation, scouts from the big English clubs began to show interest. Port Glasgow were relegated at the end of season 1908–09 and Jimmy became a transfer target.

In May 1909, Jimmy took the huge step and moved to Merseyside to sign for

Everton for a large fee, leaving behind his close-knit family and the prospect of a life in the pits. At the age of 20, and virtually the first time he had travelled any distance from his home, he could be excused for feeling slightly out of place in the urban sprawl of Merseyside. Jimmy did, however, impress everyone at Everton with his dedication, determination and will to win. He was greatly helped by the arrival of Tommy Gracie from Morton. The gifted Gracie eventually played for Hearts but was destined to die tragically with several of his Hearts' teammates in World War One. In just under four seasons at Everton, Jimmy played 54 games in a variety of positions – wing-half, inside-forward and centre-forward – scoring eight goals.

By 1913, however, Jimmy had a hankering to return home and Everton were not hard to deal with. Morton at that point were beginning to build a reputation for themselves as a club with ambition. They had just signed the English winger Stan Seymour and also had acquired the Rangers international duo of Jim Stark, who had captained Scotland in his two appearances, and John May. Jimmy Gourlay moved to Morton in May 1913. It was the start of 14 years of tremendous service in the blue and white hoops for Jimmy Gourlay.

Jimmy joined Morton just as they were building one of their best ever sides, and in his first season he made an immediate impact, scoring on his debut against Raith Rovers. Morton won their first four matches of that season, with Jimmy drawing praise for dominating matches with his personality. It soon became evident that when Gourlay played well, Morton played well. His time at Everton had served him well and he came back a confident, all-action player. He never missed a chance to shoot and generally made things happen with his strong running and eye for a goal. Morton eventually finished fourth in 1913–14, their best ever placing in the top League. A typical 'Ton side of the time contained the half-back line of Jackie Wright, Stark and May, with Jimmy at inside-right.

Jackie Wright is one of Morton's greatest ever players. He joined Morton in 1911 from Port Glasgow Juniors as a right-half but eventually found his best position as a strong, skilful centre-half. He won League caps and caps in Victory Internationals that were not recognised as official, and was a vital member of the Cup-winning side. He became Morton's manager for a spell in the 1930s and is one of the great figures in the club's history.

Jimmy Gourlay
with Everton in
1910.

The outbreak of war in September 1914 threatened to undermine the team's progress. However, Scottish football continued almost as normal with the Leagues still in place, although the Scottish Cup was suspended for the duration of the war. Jimmy soon continued with his good form and won his one and only international award in 1915 when he played inside-right for the Scottish League side against the Irish League in Belfast. He crowned the occasion with the winning goal and made the other for his former teammate at Everton, Tommy Gracie.

Surprisingly, Jimmy was never called upon again. In the same year he won his first silverware with the club when Morton won the War Shield. Eight clubs contested the tournament which was formed to raise funds for the war effort. Morton played Rangers in the Final at Firhill on 28 April 1915. Although Jimmy had established himself as one of Morton's best players, the Final belonged to English winger Stan Seymour. Seymour made one goal and scored the other in the Final in a 2–1 victory.

Everton FC, season 1911–12. A young Jimmy Gourlay is third from right, middle row. Tommy Gracie, formerly of Morton, is third from right on the front row.

Seymour was born in County Durham in 1893 and worked down the pits when, in 1911, he was given a trial by Newcastle United, the club he worshipped. He was told to come back when he had grown a few inches. He joined Bradford City and in February 1913 he reversed the popular trend and moved north to join Morton, where he became a huge star with his sparkling wing play and powerful shooting. He stayed with Morton for seven years and was an integral part of both the club and the town. He finally signed for his beloved Newcastle in 1920 for £2,000. In the ensuing 50 years, Stan Seymour became one of the most important, revered and controversial figures in the club's history as player, manager and chairman. He never lost his affection for Morton, however, maintaining a close friendship with several of his old teammates and later forming a friendship with Hal Stewart. His memories of his time with Morton were so precious to him that his home in Newcastle was christened 'Cappielow'.

Morton in 1919. Jimmy is in the front row, second from left.

Morton continued their good form throughout the war years, finishing fourth, third, second, fourth and third in successive seasons. They were one of the top clubs in Scotland and in Jimmy Gourlay possessed one of the most dedicated professionals in the country, who, in his first four seasons with Morton, scored 70 goals. The major silverware continued to elude Jimmy and Morton, however, although in a match at Cappielow in 1918, Morton beat Rangers 1–0 with a goal from Jimmy Gourlay. It would be almost 70 years before Morton next won a home League match against Rangers, but the score and the goalscorer would repeat itself long before that, and on a much grander scale. 1920 looked as if it could be Morton's year when they reached the semi-final of the Scottish Cup. They took an early 2–0 lead against Kilmarnock, but Killie fought back, eventually winning 3–2. Kilmarnock then went on to win the Final.

The same year saw a tragic event after a match against Rangers at Cappielow. The Rangers manager, William Wilton, drowned in a boating accident in Cardwell Bay, Gourock.

1922 was the year when all the promise shown by Morton finally came to fruition. The first fine side of the century had broken up, and a new side had been built. At 34, Jimmy was now considered a veteran and had moved back to right-half. He was still the fulcrum of the side, the father figure of a group of talented footballers who were about to realise their finest hour. Morton's first, and to date only, Scottish Cup Final win began against Vale of Leithen in January 1922 with a 4–0 win. The next round saw 'Ton struggle to draw with Clydebank before winning 3–1 in the replay with goals by French, Mackay and an own goal.

In the third round 'Ton hit top form beating Clyde 4–1 in a Cappielow gale, with French (two), McNab and McKay scoring. In the quarter-finals they came up against a much-fancied Motherwell side containing the famous Bobby

Greenock Morton – Scottish Cup winners in 1922.

Ferrier. It was Jimmy Gourlay who emerged as man of the match, however, with his superb tackling and covering. His display did not go unnoticed. He was being openly mentioned as a candidate for a Scotland cap despite his advancing years. The *Port Glasgow Express* was of the opinion that it was, 'The hope of a Scottish badge that is responsible for the rejuvenation of the old Clune Park favourite.' Alec Brown and George French scored for Morton in the 2–1 victory at Fir Park.

Morton had reached their second semi-final in three seasons and this time there were no slip-ups. They completely outplayed Aberdeen at Dens Park with the talismanic centre-forward George French scoring twice and Alex McNab the other in a 3–1 victory. French had now scored in every round and as much as anyone was responsible for Morton's progress to the Final. The *Greenock Telegraph* was of the opinion that French's performance stamped him as Scotland's greatest centre-forward. Cruelly, however, just as French was at the peak of his powers, injury on the eve of the Final caused him to miss Morton's greatest triumph.

The Final was played at Hampden Park on 15 April 1922 against Rangers. Morton have only ever reached four major Finals in their history and in each their opponents have been Rangers.

On the eve of the Final the *Telegraph* reported that Alex McNab, Morton's international winger, had been at the centre of a drowning incident the previous evening. McNab had been walking on Gourock's promenade when a young boy fell into a bathing pool. McNab and another passer by had pulled the boy from the water and successfully resuscitated him. The modest McNab had made no mention of the incident to his teammates.

A crowd of 75,000 made their way to Hampden on a dull, breezy day, including a sizable contingent of some 15,000 to 20,000 from the Greenock area. Greenock resembled a ghost town as the Morton fans made their way to Glasgow by every method possible, including by foot. Rangers were hot favourites despite the fact that they were in the middle of a Scottish Cup jinx. They had not won the Cup since 1903 and, in an upset the previous year, had lost to Partick Thistle in the Final. But they still boasted the best side in Scotland with greats such as Davie Meiklejohn and Alan Morton in the side. Perhaps not wanting to tempt fate, no official

Morton FC pictured in 1925. Jimmy is seated, second from the left.

celebrations had been planned by Morton. The club had even arranged to leave for a friendly against Hartlepool immediately after the match.

The teams lined up thus:

MORTON: Edwards, McIntyre, R. Brown, Gourlay, Wright, McGregor, McNab, McKay, Buchanan, A. Brown, McMinn.

RANGERS: Robb, Manderson, McCandless, Meiklejohn, Dixon, Muirhead, Archibald, Cunningham, Henderson, Cairns, Morton.

Jock Buchanan took the place of the injured French. The loss of French was a huge blow to the Greenock men. One sportswriter likened French's omission to the loss of a Wellington or Napoleon. The opening exchanges were tough with play frequently halted for injuries. The goal that earned Jimmy Gourlay immortality was scored in the 11th minute of the match when Rangers goalkeeper Willie Robb was penalised for over carrying the ball from his penalty area.

A direct free-kick was awarded and Jimmy took responsibility. The Rangers

Another photograph from 1925. Jimmy Gourlay is seated on the far right.

defenders were reluctant to retreat the necessary 10 yards, but Jimmy insisted that they move back and, displaying his customary coolness and shooting accuracy, he floated the ball over the defensive wall and high into the top corner of the net, despite a despairing effort by a Rangers defender to get his head to the ball. The *Greenock Telegraph* called the effort 'a triumph of poise and aiming' and it was the first time a goal had been scored direct from a free-kick in a Scottish Final. It would be 26 years until the next one – Jimmy Whyte of Morton against Rangers.

In the 20th minute of the match Rangers lost Andy Cunningham with a broken jaw as the match deteriorated into a tough, no-holds-barred physical contest. Rangers then piled on the pressure and tried to create openings through Alan Morton, but 'Ton's fearless right-back Jock McIntyre was more than a match and kept the star winger in check. With at least three Morton players carrying injuries, they held on until half-time. For the first 20 minutes of the second half, Morton took the game to Rangers with wingers McNab and McMinn creating several chances which could have resulted in more goals. Inevitably, the closing stages saw Rangers throw everything at the Morton defence and Morton goalie Davie Edwards emerged as the hero with some outstanding saves. By the final whistle of a tough, gruelling match several of the Morton players were walking wounded but they held on resolutely to record a famous victory.

The trophy was presented to the club chairman, W.B. McMillan. This was a poignant moment as he was to die a month later. The Morton players celebrated by drinking champagne borrowed from Queens Park and headed off by train for their match in Hartlepool on the Monday. On arrival in Hartlepool, the victorious Morton party were escorted to their hotel by a deputation of Hartlepool officials and townspeople whilst being serenaded by the town band. On return to Greenock a huge crowd of fans had gathered at Greenock Central railway station, and several members of the side left the train at other stations to 'avoid the ordeal of a public demonstration'. However, the club's next home game saw 10,000 fans gather at Cappielow to watch their heroes take the field holding the Cup aloft. After the match there was a mini pitch invasion and goalkeeper Davie Edwards was carried shoulder high from the field.

The winning of the Scottish Cup quite obviously stands as Morton Football Club's greatest achievement in their history. It is fitting that a man like Jimmy Gourlay should be the person who more than anyone made it possible. Primitive footage exists of the Final, but unfortunately it consists of little more than the players running out on to the field and around one minute of action where it is virtually impossible to identify any of the players.

With Morton finally winning the major trophy that their good form of the preceding 10 years deserved, it seemed as if they had finally made the big breakthrough. But just as they seemed on the cusp of greater things, the side was broken up, and the club entered a downward spiral that took years to arrest. Jimmy soldiered on, a reliable presence as Morton toiled in the lower half of the League. Jimmy's last season as a player was 1926–27, which ended in relegation for the club after 27 successive seasons in the top League. Jimmy was now 38 years old and had one last final fling with a dozen games with Third Lanark before retiring aged 39.

It had been a glorious career and Jimmy's love for Morton had grown immeasurably over the years. Throughout his time at Morton he remained modest about his achievements, but one thing he did enjoy was whenever he was at Ibrox during Rangers' barren spell, when they went 25 years without winning the Scottish Cup. According to Bob Crampsey he would prime Bob McPhail, the famous Rangers inside-forward of the time, who had won a cup medal with Airdrie, to ask him what he had in his pocket. Jimmy would produce his Cup-winners' medal and McPhail would say, 'Oh yes, they tell me there's not too many of them around here', much to the annoyance of the Rangers players.

After he retired Jimmy was offered a coaching position in Sweden, which he took up with the intention of sending for his family when he had settled in. Before this could happen, however, he grew homesick and returned home to work in the shipyards.

He was a regular visitor to Cappielow and a member of the Supporters Club and it was through the club that he met Jimmy Davies. Davies was the manager of the

The Morton 1922 Cup-winning side reunited in a veterans' match in 1938. Jimmy Gourlay is second from the left, front row.

Jimmy Gourlay in his later role as trainer (standing extreme right) in 1947.

short-lived but successful Morton Juniors side of the 1930s and he invited Jimmy to join as trainer. Davies became the Morton manager in 1939 and before long Jimmy joined him at Cappielow as trainer. It was the beginning of one of the most exciting periods in Morton's history. It was a period that witnessed an assembly line of internationals at the club, culminating in another Scottish Cup Final appearance in 1948. It was in his position as trainer that Jimmy Gourlay cemented his enduring reputation as one of the greatest figures in Morton's history.

He was a constant fixture at the club, always on hand to dispense wisdom, provide a welcoming ear or administer a rollicking when required. He became known as the father of the team and would carry his little black kitbag around with him, although whether it contained anything more than the standard 'magic' sponge is anyone's guess. Always a pragmatic man, he did not suffer fools gladly and told it like it was, but was a friend when needed. It was his relationship with players like

Billy Steel and Jimmy Cowan that helped them become the great players that they were. Defeat in the 1948 Scottish Cup Final only heightened Jimmy's ambition to see Morton win major silverware again, but Morton were relegated in 1952 and were to spend the rest of Jimmy's time at Cappielow struggling in the old Second Division. Through it all Jimmy remained the same resolute, cheerful person, and it did not seem to matter which ground Morton visited, there was always an old foe or acquaintance for him to talk to about old times.

Jimmy retired as trainer in 1959, aged 70. He was made an honorary member of the club and tributes were warm and heartfelt. The great goalkeeper Jimmy Cowan said of Jimmy:

It was largely due to Jimmy Gourlay that I was able to do as well as a goalkeeper. Jimmy was more than a trainer. He was like a father and his constant cheerfulness always succeeded in raising the players for the game.

The *Greenock Telegraph* commented, 'So long as football is talked about in these parts one name will never fail to be mentioned when the triumphs and disasters of Greenock Morton are surveyed. The name is Jimmy Gourlay, the man who scored the goal that won the Cup.'

Bert Gourlay, a powerful and talented inside-forward, spent the whole of the 1950s at Cappielow. Bert was Jimmy's nephew, but there was no favouritism showed by Jimmy.

Jimmy was very strict with training, and he didn't do me any favours because I was his nephew. He insisted that the players behaved the rules, and he hated swearing, he wouldn't allow it. He was a good motivator and a good listener, and quite modest about his achievements. As well as football he was a great bowler and won a lot of championships.

After his retirement, Jimmy continued to attend games and continued with his bowling. He was a keen Burnsian and a committed family man with three daughters. He lived in the street just behind his beloved Cappielow, and it was in his home that he died in September 1970, aged 82. There was a minute's silence and the Morton flag flew at half-mast the following Saturday at Cappielow against Dundee United, a match that Morton fittingly won. The *Greenock Telegraph* reminisced about Jimmy's goal against Rangers and said, 'In the clash of great events it may seem a small thing, but the life of a small community depends upon personal values and proud recollections.' No one epitomised these qualities more than Jimmy Gourlay – the original Mr Morton.

Morton playing statistics: (League and Scottish Cup)

Season	Appearances	Goals
1913–14	31	15
1914–15	35	23
1915–16	30	18
1916–17	33	14
1917–18	25	6
1918–19	23	6
1919–20	40	9
1920–21	31	9
1921–22	30	3
1922–23	29	5
1923–24	35	6
1924–25	36	2
1925–26	28	4
1926–27	20	4

Chapter 2

Billy Steel
The Blonde Bombshell

Confidence is a big factor in football. The pages of football history are littered with the players who were 'nearly men' – they had all the talent, but lacked that extra special belief in their ability that could take them to greater heights. Of the many criticisms that can be levelled at Billy Steel, a lack of confidence certainly was not amongst them. This was the man who authored a book at the age of 25, called *How to Play Football*. Never was a title more appropriate as Billy spent his entire career telling people – mostly teammates – how to play football. If this did not exactly endear him to some of his colleagues, Billy's inherent confidence was overwhelmingly justified. Billy Steel was quite simply one of the greatest players Scotland has ever produced. He came from the long tradition of Scottish inside-forwards. Small, stocky and tricky with a fiery temper, he was the natural successor to the great Alex James.

Billy Steel was born in 1923 in the Stirlingshire village of Denny. The street in which he was born had form. Jimmy McMullan, who captained the famous Wembley Wizards Scotland side in 1928, was also born there. Billy was something of a child prodigy, his talent there for all to see. His name was known far beyond his close-knit community. He won his first schoolboy cap aged 13 alongside George Young, who would later become one of Rangers' greatest ever players. The two young boys formed a firm and lasting friendship, and Young would be Steel's Scotland skipper on many occasions. Billy's diminutive size as a schoolboy earned him the soubriquet 'Wee Wullie'. Hardly original, but Billy was certainly not the last small Scottish footballer to be anointed as such. At 14 he signed for juvenile side Dunipace Thistle, and in 1938, aged 15, he signed for junior side Bo'ness Cadora. Billy's displays for Bo'ness attracted senior attention and he was soon snapped up by Leicester City. After a few months, however, he grew homesick and managed to secure his release from Leicester and returned to Scotland and signed for St Mirren in May 1939 as an amateur. He made his first-team debut for St Mirren against Rangers on his 16th birthday. A lot had happened to Billy in a very short space of time, and perhaps it was too much for someone so young. Initially he struggled at St Mirren before finding his form again.

But just as they would do a few years later with Jimmy Cowan, St Mirren contrived to allow one of Scotland's greatest ever players slip though their fingers to join their fierce county rivals. As he approached his 17th birthday, Billy was still registered as an amateur with St Mirren. While Saints dallied, Morton, in the shape of wily manager Jimmy Davies, stepped in and offered Billy professional terms on his 17th birthday, the age at which he was allowed to sign as a professional. Billy signed for Morton in May 1940 for the princely signing on fee of £50. It was a watershed for both the club and Billy himself. Up until he signed for 'Ton, Billy had

been a bit of a lost soul, drifting from club to club. With Morton he found somewhere that his talents could be given free rein. Morton and Billy were good for one another, and it was at Cappielow that he truly began to blos-

Billy with Morton in 1942. He is seated second from the right.

som and make a name for himself. Billy would say in later years that joining Morton was one of the best football decisions he ever made.

The early 1940s saw the beginning of one of the most productive eras in Morton's history with some of the club's finest ever players signing during this period. Billy Campbell and Tommy Orr, local boys destined to become two of Morton's greatest players, signed in 1941 and 1942 respectively, and Jimmy Cowan was still to come. Although World War Two was in full swing there was a League programme in place, albeit somewhat truncated and lacking some of its stars who had been called up. A new Cup competition, the Southern League Cup (which would later evolve into the League Cup) was also introduced, and Morton reached the Final in 1942. There they lost 1–0 to Rangers. The match was notable for Billy playing the entire match in severe pain – he was rushed to hospital immediately after the match for an emergency appendix operation – and for it being Billy's last before joining the Army. Still not quite 19, Billy joined the Royal Signal Corps, volunteering before he was called up. He had a sympathetic commanding officer who loved football and Billy continued to turn out for Morton whenever he could, and his star continued to rise. He was helped by the astute Davies, and the calm and thoughtful trainer Jimmy Gourlay, who became something of a mentor to Billy.

In November 1942, Cappielow hosted a match between the British and Dutch army sides, and predictably, Billy took the honours with two goals as the British side, which included the famous Chelsea and Hearts star Tommy Walker, romped home 8–0.

A typical Morton side of that period would read: McFeat, Maley and Fyfe, Aird, Gray and Campbell, Adams, Orr, Crum, Steel and Kelly. There was also the young Jimmy Garth, who was just breaking through, and the elegant John Divers was also a regular. Manager Jimmy Davies was building good sides that unfortunately always seemed to end up the bridesmaids. The pattern continued for Billy up until 1944, when Billy landed in France with the Royal Signal Corps. Sporadic games for Morton were interspersed with his appearances for the Army side. The importance of the Army matches to the morale of troops and civilians alike should not be underestimated. The matches raised valuable funds for the war effort, and gave troops and fans alike respite from the demands of the war. Morton enjoyed a

Billy Steel on Scotland duty with the great Jimmy Mason of Third Lanark.

particularly good season in 1942–43, eventually finishing runners-up to Rangers in the League. Who knows what they could have achieved if they had not been denied the talents of Steel for so many matches?

Billy spent the last two years of the war travelling all over Europe playing for the British Army On The Rhine side. He would later remember this period as, 'Nothing unusual, just a few games of football with the section.' This was a considerable understatement as he did see action on the Rhine.

Billy was demobbed just before Christmas 1946 and immediately rejoined Morton. For Morton fans at the end of the war, a proper League programme could

STEEL

A cigarette card featuring Billy Steel, dating from 1947.

not come soon enough with the prospect of Steel, and his wing partner Johnny Kelly, and experienced campaigners such as Johnny Crum and John Divers teaming up with the three players who would become Morton's great triumvirate – Cowan, Campbell and Orr. However, a combination of circumstances would ensure that the 'dream team' would play together on sadly too few occasions.

Crum's career drew to a close before the end of the war, and fellow ex-Celt Divers suffered a series of injuries that seriously impaired his Morton career, causing him to miss the 1948 Cup Final. Kelly was transferred to Barnsley at the end of the war, and Billy Steel? Billy was also bound for England. Basically, his talent was too all-encompassing for a side like Morton. He had won his first cap for Scotland in April 1947 against England at Wembley in a match Scotland had been tipped to lose heavily. The match ended 1–1 and the English newspapers were full of praise for Billy's inspirational performance. Lifelong Morton supporter Arthur Montford was at Wembley that day and his memories of the match are still vivid. 'I had thrilled to the sight a year earlier of watching Billy Campbell play against England at Hampden, and I must confess there was a lump in my throat as I watched Billy Steel make the long walk out of the Wembley tunnel.'

Billy's performance in the England match led to him being named in the Great Britain XI against a Rest of Europe select at Hampden Park in May 1947. The

Greenock Telegraph boasted that they were the first to break the news of his inclusion to Billy. Billy told the paper, 'I am certainly surprised and delighted but any success I have had is down to my teammates at Cappielow. The honour is as much theirs as mine.' The same reporter observed that Steel's departure in the near future was a certainty, and wondered what the psychological effect might be on two other stars at Cappielow: Billy Campbell and Tommy Orr.

Billy knew that this match was his chance to put himself in the transfer shop window. In a mouth-watering forward line that read Matthews, Mannion, Lawton, Steel and Liddell, Billy in no way looked out of place. The 'Blond Bombshell' had arrived. The match ended 6–1 for Great Britain against a side that could only tenuously be regarded as the best the rest of Europe could put out. If the one-sided match had not quite lived up to its billing as 'the match of the century', and despite the questionable quality of the opposition, Billy Steel stood out as one of the classiest players on the field, scoring one goal and making another two. It was this match and Billy's performance that effectively made Billy's eventual transfer from Morton inevitable.

His goal is justly regarded as one of the finest ever scored at Hampden. With the match nicely poised at 2–1 to Britain, Billy picked the ball up in the centre circle and threaded his way past three defenders before unleashing a 20-yard left-foot shot that flew into the net with tremendous power and unerring accuracy. It says something of the impact that Billy Steel had made in football when he was selected for this match. He had only been demobbed from the army just before Christmas 1946 and had managed just 12 appearances for Morton in the whole of the 1946–47 season. But his brilliant display at Wembley against the English was the turning point of his career, and undoubtedly led to him being picked for the Great Britain side. Billy had of course played with Matthews and Lawton when they had 'guested' for Morton during the war, and he now knew that he was playing to their standards. Arthur Montford was by now making something of a habit of catching Billy's reputation-making performances. He attended the Hampden match along with future Morton chairman, Douglas Rae, and both men acknowledged that they had witnessed the birth of a star, and precipitously observed that Billy would soon be moving up the football ladder.

If modern day football has a convoluted transfer system with agents and advisors involved at every stage, then Steel's transfer saga was the most talked about subject in football in the spring of 1947. The war changed many people's lives in a way that they were powerless to stop. But Billy decided to take control of his own life and destiny. Up until now, he had played more or less for the love of the game, but now he wished to maximise his talent. His oft-stated ambition was to earn at least £20,000 from football before he retired. Billy returned from the war a changed man. His performance for the Great Britain XI and his Scotland debut at Wembley only served to convince him that his talents deserved a grander stage and a better reward. There was also some unrest at Cappielow amongst some of the Morton

Billy with the Great Britain XI in 1947. He is second right, flanked by Wilf Mannion and Stanley Matthews.

players over Billy's domineering attitude, which was beginning to surface for the first time.

Three clubs – Wolves, Middlesbrough and reigning League champions Liverpool – entered a bidding war with both Liverpool and Boro offering £12,500. Billy rather enigmatically said, 'I believe one or two clubs would like to have me, but if you want to know who they are you will have to talk to Mr Davies.' The transfer saga rolled on like a soap opera. Liverpool bid £15,000 and then withdrew the bid. The size of the projected fee was questioned with one reporter asking, 'If Steel is worth £15,000, what price Alex James and Bob McPhail?'

Billy joined the Scotland continental touring party right in the middle of the transfer speculation. On 18 May he won his second cap against Belgium, scoring Scotland's goal in a 2–1 defeat, and then starred in a 6–0 victory over Luxembourg on 24 May. Billy scored twice against Luxembourg bringing his total to three goals in three matches for Scotland as a Morton player. There would be no more caps in a Morton jersey but for the man in the size five boots there would be fame and fortune, and not a little controversy, in the ensuing years. Unknown to everyone apart from Billy, Derby County, flush with money having just won the FA Cup in 1946, had been tracking the situation. In early June 1947, Morton accepted their bid of £15,500. It was claimed to be a world record transfer fee, and was certainly the biggest fee ever paid between two British clubs. Although Morton have been criticised throughout their history for selling their best players, they really had no option with Steel. He had outgrown the club and had to follow his destiny, but did Morton see the best of Billy? Bob Crampsey thinks Billy only blossomed when he left Cappielow.

I think it's fair to say that Morton, because of a combination of circumstances, didn't see the best of Billy Steel. His best performances as a Morton player probably came at international level where he made a huge impact in a short space of time.

The bare statistics – 12 official matches and three goals – only scratch the surface of Billy Steel's career at Morton. The impact he made during the war years convinced the Morton fans that he was a star in the making, and for a Morton player

A signed portrait of Billy from his time with Derby County.

to play in the same forward line as Matthews, Lawton et al was a tremendous boost for the club.

With Derby, Billy now had the grand stage that he had desired for so long. Behind the choirboy's face lay a driven man. He was a perfectionist and he sought riches from the game. When others did not meet his exacting requirements, he was not slow to give them a rollicking on the field. He had a vicious tongue and his caustic comments did not endear him to his new Derby teammates, especially as he took his time to find his own form. When eventually he did find his form, his individual brilliance was staggering, but trophies eluded Derby. During his time at Derby, Billy decided that he wanted to live and train in Glasgow, and only travel down to Derby for games. He even held a press conference to put forward his point of view. Such actions were unheard of in football at that time, and a weary Derby decided that Steel should go. His great Scotland form continued unabated throughout the hullabaloo – he remained an automatic choice for his country. When he left Derby, their fans were divided over Billy Steel. Most recognised they had witnessed a genius, but were unsure as to the off-field baggage.

If some of Billy's Derby teammates did not recognise his gifts, then many of his opponents certainly did. For Sir Tom Finney, who played against Billy many times at club level and in five home internationals, Billy was an exceptional footballer.

Oh, Billy was well respected by the English. He was a force to be reckoned with. He had everything really – two good feet, very sharp on the ball and good in the air for his size. Because he was so small, that low centre of gravity allowed him to move away from opponents with ease. He had the gift of being two moves ahead of other players. And of course he was a fiery little character, and he had that great confidence, arrogance even. Yes, I have fond memories of those England-Scotland matches, and when Billy played, Scotland always seemed to do well.

Billy signed for Dundee in 1950 for yet another record fee of £23,500 and, for the first time at club level, fully lived up to his reputation. He returned to Cappielow for the first time in September that year to face his old side, much changed from his days there. Morton led 2–0, but a virtuoso second-half performance by Steel turned the match around, and Dundee won 3–2. But controversy seemed to follow Billy around.

He became the first Scotland player to be sent off when he was given an early bath against Austria in Vienna in 1951. In a rough house of a match, he was ordered off after an innocuous clash with an opponent. On his way off the park, as 65,000 Austrians bayed for blood, he was unceremoniously kicked up the backside by an Austrian fan resplendent in full lederhosen and jackboots! An enraged Steel had to be dragged away by five policemen.

With Dundee, Billy won the League Cup twice, but major success eluded him. He did however seal his reputation as the most skilful Scottish footballer of the post-war years. But the restless Steel only managed three glory years at Dundee before once more deciding to move on. This time it was permanent. In dispute with Dundee, he decided to emigrate to the United States in 1954. An ankle injury had limited his powers and, ever the perfectionist, Billy decided that if he could not play at his peak then he would not play at all. He had won 30 caps and scored 12 goals. Dundee held onto his registration until 1956 when they finally officially freed him. By this time Billy had pursued a new career in newspapers. He had played for a while in Los Angeles before retiring and becoming a reporter, expressing himself as forcibly in print as he did on the football field. He eventually became a powerful newspaper executive and settled in California until his death in 1982, aged only 59.

Did Billy Steel achieve everything he could have in football? The answer must be no. His story is similar to so many Scottish footballers from Hughie Gallacher to Jim Baxter – a brilliant glowing comet destined to crash and burn. Without doubt his wilful nature prevented him from achieving the greatness his huge talent

Billy Steel trots off the field after being sent off while playing for Scotland.

deserved. He played for good sides but never really played with the great players at club level that he encountered playing with Scotland. Lawrie Reilly, despite being a centre-forward for Hibs, was Billy's favoured wing partner.

Billy reckoned I was the best winger he had played with because I was just a young lad with plenty of energy, so it was natural for me to switch inside. This would give Billy a wee rest and bamboozle defenders into the bargain.

Lawrie remembers Billy as the most confident player he had ever known.

Well to have that much confidence in your own ability is no bad thing. It was Billy's greatest asset in fact. It allowed Billy to do things others wouldn't have tried. And for a wee man he was very strong. He had a good physique and was good in the air for his size.

How will time remember Billy Steel? He was a fans' player. Everywhere he went the fans loved him. He was a law unto himself, a forerunner of the hard-nosed footballer that would eventually become the norm. He had a natural fitness with unorthodox gymnastic-style training methods. One of his party pieces was walking the length of the pitch on his hands. His low centre of gravity made him almost impossible to dispossess and, like Dalglish 25 years later, Billy was often two or three moves ahead of his teammates.

Towards the end of his life Billy contacted Arthur Montford to ask if Arthur could contact some of his old teammates with Morton and Scotland for a reunion. Arthur

Billy Steel, at the height of his fame and besieged by autograph hunters, is pictured while with Dundee in 1952.

was delighted to oblige and Willie Woodburn of Rangers and George Mitchell of Morton were just two of his old friends who spent time with him. Arthur also made a tape of Billy's games which both touched and delighted him.

Billy had one other Morton connection. Before Hal Stewart came to Morton he had an association with Dundee Football Club thanks to his friendship with Billy's manager at the time, George Anderson. After he came to Morton in the 1960s, Hal would often wax lyrical about Billy. For Hal Stewart, Billy was one of the finest players he had ever seen. Commenting on his death in 1982, Hal paid this simple tribute, 'We have lost one of the all-time greats.'

No one who saw Billy Steel play could argue with that assessment. Billy concluded his book *How To Play Football* by saying his proudest moment was when he donned his blue Scotland jersey to battle against England at Wembley in 1947. For many Morton fans of the time that was their proudest moment – Billy Steel of Scotland – and Morton.

Morton playing statistics: (League and Scottish Cup)

Season	Appearances	Goals
1946–47	12	3

Chapter 3

Erik Sorensen
The Man in Black

In the 21st century 'free economy', footballers are free to move from country to country, and continent to continent, and seemingly embrace their newly adopted home with ease. However, perhaps we should pause to think back to a player who was very much a pioneer. Erik Sorensen was not the first Scandinavian footballer to play in Scotland when he signed for Morton in 1964. Rangers for one had a Dane – Carl Hansen who signed in 1921 – but Erik was most certainly the highest profile of what would become known as the 'Scandinavian Invasion' of the 1960s. Many talented footballers from Scandinavia followed in his wake. But back in 1964, it was very much an alien concept for 'foreigners' to sign for a Scottish club. It must have been a daunting prospect for a young man to leave his homeland and uproot his family to settle in sunny Greenock. But Erik adapted admirably, thanks to his great talent as a goalkeeper and his great strength of character. So much so, that when his professional football career ended, Erik remained a popular figure, and continued to live and work in the town. Indeed he was to return to Morton as manager.

Erik Lykke (Lykke is Danish for lucky) Sorensen was born in Odense in Denmark in 1940. In the same year the Nazis invaded his country, and Erik's earliest memories are indelibly linked to the occupation of his country by Hitler's forces.

I can remember as a small child, the Gestapo storming the tenements, looking for members of the Resistance. It has always amazed me at how inventive those people were in finding hiding places. However, every so often they would find someone like my own father who was a member of the Resistance. He was sent to the concentration camps, but managed to escape en route. I then didn't see him for many months, but then suddenly one night he was there again in our home. Like everyone else during the war we were very poor, but things started to look up after the war and I began to take part in sports. My father was a boxer and a goalie too, and I loved boxing, so I guess I must have inherited my natural talent from him. Initially I played outfield but, when I was about 13 or 14, I began to play in goal for the Odense B1909 youth side. I stayed with them until I was about 19, and won a Danish championship medal.

Army national service then interrupted Erik's career, but he continued to play for the Odense B1909 club and won another championship medal. Erik left the army in 1961 and moved to the other major club in Odense, B1913, where he swiftly began to forge his reputation. The 'B' in the Danish club names is short for Boldklubben, which means football club, and the figures (1909 and 1913) are the years when the particular clubs were founded. He won the Danish Cup with B1913 and made his full international debut against Romania in 1963.

By early 1964, Erik had won eight under-23 and 10 full caps. He had played in the European Cup against Real Madrid so, despite his amateur status, Erik was a very experienced goalkeeper. All football in Denmark at this time was amateur, but it really was amateur in name only, as the players were tremendously skilful, and professional in their outlook. This would swiftly become apparent when Denmark reached the semi-final of the European Championships of 1964. 'Despite our amateur status the Danish national side was one of the best in Europe. Within a year of reaching the semi-final, almost the whole side signed professionally for teams all over Europe.'

Erik earned the nickname 'Tarzan' in his country thanks to his daily training and fitness regime. He also earned the nickname 'The Black Panther' for his habit of playing in all black and his almost cat-like agility. The goalkeeper Erik admired most was the great Russian, Lev Yashin.

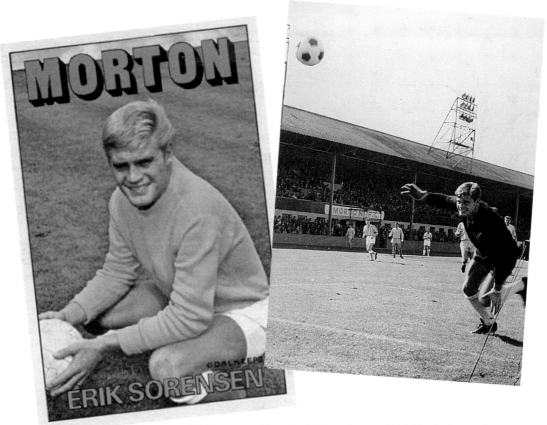

Erik Sorensen pictured in 1965 and on a collectable Morton card.

I studied the best goalies and learned good techniques from coaches in Denmark, who were years ahead of their time, and I worked hard to improve my game. I liked to wear an all black strip just to be different from the run-of-the-mill yellow jersey.

The events that changed Erik's and many other Danish footballers' lives forever were put in motion by a friendly match at Cappielow in 1964 against Danish club Bronshoj of Copenhagen, who included future Morton players Preben Arentoft and Borge Thorup in their line-up. The Bronshoj goalkeeper, Arne Nielsen, put up a terrific performance and Hal Stewart offered to sign him. However, the player's manager told Hal that the goalie had just played the game of his life, and actually was not a particularly good goalie. Hal was told that the man Morton should sign was actually Erik Sorensen, the current Danish national goalie.

Erik in action, displaying his popular acrobatic style.

By the end of 1963, I knew it was inevitable that I would be leaving Denmark to go abroad in the spring. There was interest from clubs in Germany and Bilbao in Spain. An English club was also keen and my mother was English, but the English had a ruling that you had to be resident in Britain for two years before you could sign for an English club. In those days though, money came second as long as you and your family were happy. I was informed of Morton's interest and I met Hal Stewart in the old Renfrew Airport Hotel. I liked Hal from the first moment I saw him even though he tried a wee dodge with my contract. He offered me a two-year contract and I looked at the sum of money and told him to add at least one zero, and he agreed immediately. 'Oh, that's no problem', he said. He really was the last of a dying breed.

Erik arrived in Scotland in March 1964, by which time Morton had already won the Second Division championship with their record-breaking side. At the time Erik had not even heard of Greenock never mind Morton. Dundee and Rangers were the only Scottish clubs that he knew anything about. Hal, being the master publicist, could not let the opportunity of capitalising on the signing of a six-foot blond Viking pass. Allan McGraw played in Erik's debut, a friendly against Third Lanark, and remembers Hal telling the players that they were to tell the press only that Erik was fresh from the Liverpool docks. Against Third Lanark, Erik took to the field in an all black strip and was immediately dubbed 'The Man in Black' by the press.

The *Daily Record* also posed the question: 'Morton's Mr 'X' – Who is He?' It was yet another masterful public relations coup from Hal Stewart, ensuring that Morton's name was in the papers yet again for all the right reasons. Jim Rodger of the *Record* reported that Morton fans had been plunged into mystery over the identity of the star goalkeeper, whose excellent display had denied Thirds several goals. It is hard to imagine nowadays a friendly match between two small Scottish clubs attracting such interest, but anything and everything was big news at Morton under the magic wand of Hal Stewart. The match ended in a draw, and as a further sign of the times, the Third Lanark players each won a transistor radio as their prize for winning the match on a toss of the coin. Erik remembers the veil of secrecy regarding his debut and how Hal Stewart orchestrated it in typical fashion. 'I was introduced to the rest of the players only as "Eric" because the big secret was to be kept for a few more days.'

However, it was impossible to keep it a secret, and after the match Hal Stewart said that he believed Erik could go on to become one of the biggest personalities in Scottish football. The following day's *Greenock Telegraph* carried the headline 'Cloak of Mystery Falls From Hero of Cathkin' as in yet another great public relations exercise, a Morton insider revealed that Erik was a national sporting hero in Denmark and had turned down offers from Barcelona and Juventus to join Morton.

A few days later 10,000 intrigued fans watched Erik's League debut at Cappielow against Alloa. It was not the best of starts for Erik as a misunderstanding with centre-half Jim Kiernan led to an Alloa goal. Erik featured in a chapter of the *Scottish Football Book* of 1965 and he told the editor, Hugh Taylor, that the misunderstanding was down to his habit of coming right out of his goal area to clear the ball. On many occasions this would involve going outside the 18-yard line.

Scottish defenders of the time were not used to goalkeepers acting as an auxiliary 'sweeper' and this caused the confusion with Jim Kiernan.

However, it was a minor blip for Erik and by the beginning of season 1964–65, with 'Ton back in the top League, he had established himself as Morton's number one. Unfortunately for Erik, and new Morton teammate, fellow Dane Kaj Johansen, the timing of their transfers to Morton coincided with Denmark qualifying for the European Nations Finals tournament of 1964. Incredible as it may seem now, the Danish Football Association had taken the decision to exclude professional players from the national side. So, by dint of signing for Morton, Erik and Kaj were denied the opportunity to play in the Danish side that reached the last four of the tournament.

It was a big disappointment to miss the Finals, but it was more important to be happy and I was very happy in Scotland. My daughter was born three months after we arrived and my family settled straight away, and that made everything much easier.

Erik is congratulated by his Morton teammates after saving a penalty in a Cup tie against Hearts.

But Denmark's loss was Morton's gain, and very soon others would follow in the duo's footsteps. Kaj Johansen, a superb full-back, signed just after Erik, playing the last three matches of the 1963–64 season. Other clubs soon followed suit, and by the end of 1965 there were Scandinavian players at several clubs. For example, Dundee United had the impressive Finn Dossing and Sweden's Orjan Persson. Aberdeen signed the fine half-back Jens Pedersen and Hearts had the fast and tricky Norwegian winger Roald Jensen. Clubs like Morton and Dundee United soon realised the value of signing these players and moving them on for a profit, with Rangers being the most eager to buy. Morton were able to attract the best of the Danish players (it was actually a Danish invasion in Greenock) and would eventually sell Johansen and Jorn Sorensen as well as Erik to Rangers, who also signed Persson from United. For the players themselves, it offered an opportunity to make a living from football.

Erik initially had some language problems, especially with one particular referee who actually thought Erik was swearing at him, when he was in fact only shouting at his teammates! 'There were some difficulties at first, but everyone at the club did their best to help me settle in. It's hard to single anyone out, but I made many good friends, and John Boyd in particular was very kind and helpful.'

It really is impossible to overstate the impact that Erik had on Morton fans and Scottish football in general. Allan McGraw feels that the impression that Erik made cannot be underestimated.

Erik was the first goalie in my experience that treated the goalkeeping position as a specialist position. Previously with Morton, goalies would just train with the rest of the players and maybe have a few shots hammered in against them. But Erik was a breath of fresh air. He was the hardest-working goalkeeper I've ever known. He was so thorough in his preparation for a game and in training he worked so hard, and was very disciplined. He would work his angles out thoroughly, and he was also one of the first goalies to throw the ball out, preferring to throw rather than kick. He was very athletic, had good reactions and could be very spectacular. He gave his defence confidence. When he first joined us, we were running away with the League and basically attacked all the time, so he wasn't called into action all that often. But when he was, his concentration and discipline was so good, and that enabled him to make vital saves. That to me is the sign of a good goalkeeper.

Erik quickly made himself a fans' favourite with some outstanding and flamboyant displays. Erik himself thinks that his main strengths were his reading of the game, and his speed off his line. His first full season at Cappielow was a good one for the club as they settled quickly into a rhythm with a side very much strengthened from the previous season. Jorn Sorensen, for many Morton fans the classiest of all the Danes, signed from French club Metz. In a departure from the usual practice, Jorn was already a professional playing in the French League, and had been capped for the French League side not long before. A fee of £15,000 secured his services, but Morton would still make a profit when they moved Jorn on to Rangers the following season.

In April 1965, Jorn and Kai Johansen were given the great honour of playing in Stanley Matthews' testimonial match. Both Danes represented a European select that included players such as Yashin, Puskas and Di Stefano. It was a tremendous boost to the reputation of both players and the prestige of Morton Football Club. Another Dane, Flemming Nielsen, arrived from Italian side Atalanta. Nielsen was yet another class player and his signing showed that Hal Stewart was attempting to move the club to another level. The large pool of players at Cappielow ensured there was also a strong reserve side that finished runners-up to Rangers in the reserve league. An eventual 10th position in the League and another trip to Hampden for a semi-final against Celtic augured well for the future, but any hopes 'Ton fans had of a second League Cup Final appearance in a row were dashed against Celtic who won 2–0. Erik had an inspired match and pulled off some outstanding saves, enhancing his reputation further.

The same season witnessed one of the most talked about and controversial matches ever seen at Cappielow and most of the action seemed to revolve around Erik's Danish teammate Carl Bertlesen. In this incredible match, Morton trailed 3–0 to Celtic with 12 minutes left. Bertlesen pulled a goal back and then Hugh Strachan made it 3–2, before Bertlesen equalised with an acrobatic overhead kick. The Morton fans were going wild roaring Morton on, when in the last minute

Morton FC in 1965. From left to right, back row: J. Boyd, J. Mallon, E. Sorensen, B. Gray, H. Strachan, E. Smith. Front row: A. McIntyre, A. McGraw, J. Graham, J. Sorensen, M. Stevenson.

Eric Smith hoisted a free-kick into the Celtic goalmouth and Bertlesen rammed it into the net, amidst bedlam as everyone in the ground believed it to be the winning goal. It was then noticed that the referee was pointing to his watch and waving his arms in the air. Amid much confusion it eventually transpired that the referee had blown for full-time just before Bertlesen's shot entered the net. The fall out over this disallowed goal threatened to relegate the death of Winston Churchill to the inside pages of the newspapers. Today, ask any Morton fan who was at the match and they will tell you that Morton were robbed of a famous victory that day.

I had some good performances against Celtic; we almost seemed to play them every week. I always got a good reception from their fans. I can remember them applauding me during a match and singing my name, and I was thinking 'this shouldn't be happening' and in fact Celtic were interested in me just before I moved to Rangers.

With all the good players at their disposal it was even more puzzling therefore that Morton struggled throughout the 1965–66 season. Hal Stewart did not get it right all the time and probably sold off too many players at the one time, resulting in an unsettled side. A typical Morton side of 1966 would contain less than half the players from the one that played throughout the 1964–65 season. An injury-laden season ended in relegation with the ultimate insult – St Mirren drawing their last game to finish one point above 'Ton and surviving in the top League. Hal Stewart vowed that Morton would bounce back and he was true to his word. Allan McGraw left, but Joe Mason and Joe Harper struck up a great partnership and Morton won the second division at a canter.

Hal Stewart promised Morton fans that this time the club would be ready for the demands of the first division – and then promptly sold their star 'keeper! Rangers had been having goalkeeping problems, and Erik signed for them in August 1967 for £30,000. The transfer of Erik to Rangers caused much consternation among Morton fans, with Hal Stewart coming in for much criticism. After selling so many star players in his tenure as Cappielow chief, Hal had promised that there would be no more as he was determined to build a side capable of European football. For many fans, Erik's transfer was one too many, but Hal countered that he could not stop Erik moving to a club like Rangers and furthering his career. Erik joined up with another big money signing at Ibrox, one Alex Ferguson who had just moved from Dunfermline for £65,000. Interestingly, their Ibrox careers would also end with being transfer listed on the same day.

Erik was a regular for Rangers in his first season, playing 47 matches in all, but lost his place in the starting line up at the beginning of season 1968–69 and spent two seasons in the reserves without playing a single first-team match. It was a huge disappointment to lose his place, and with Rangers toiling against the great Celtic side of the time, Ibrox was not a particularly happy place to be.

I didn't really settle at Rangers even though it was a great experience for me. The first season went well, but then I lost my place, and I was unable to get back in. I didn't really like all the baggage that is associated with playing for the Old Firm either.

During his time with Rangers, Erik, with an eye to the future, bought the well-known Cottage Bar in Greenock, and also engaged in several other business ventures. 'Sorensens', as the pub came to be known, became a busy and popular pub and Erik remained there for more than a decade. Erik was eventually put on the transfer list at Ibrox along with Alex Ferguson, and he was offered the chance to return to Morton. Erik rejoined Morton in August 1970 initially as back up for fellow Dane, Leif Neilsen. Erik did not have to wait too long to reclaim his place as Morton's first choice goalkeeper. The brilliant Leif Neilsen was unfortunately injury prone and, by early 1971, Erik was first choice goalkeeper again.

It was great to be back at Cappielow. I had really missed the fans and especially Haldane Y Stewart. He is certainly one man that I am happy to have known. He had a great knowledge of football and a great sense of humour. I remember a reporter was trying to make a joke of Hal's transfer dealings, and he asked Hal what was the best sale he ever made and Hal replied, 'Well I once sold someone a load of racing pigeons'.

Erik's return to Morton coincided with the Danish FA rethinking their stance on overseas players and in 1971 they decided to allow players playing abroad to represent their country again. Erik's good form at Morton had not gone unnoticed and he was recalled to the Danish squad after an absence of seven years – against surprise, surprise Scotland. In a match in Copenhagen in 1971, Erik became the first Morton player to be capped for almost 20 years. To his great pride and delight Denmark won 1–0 against his adopted homeland. Also in the team were Brian Laudrup's father Finn, and Erik's old teammate at Cappielow, Preben Arentoft. Erik went on to win another four caps as a Morton player, and enjoyed two productive seasons at Cappielow as the number one goalkeeper.

Erik had hit a rich vein of form and was an ever present in season 1971–72. He began the following season again in outstanding form, playing in the first 10 matches of the League campaign, before he was laid low by injury and illness. In Erik's time most clubs liked to have two decent goalkeepers at their disposal and, with Leif Nielsen gone, Morton had signed Roy Baines from Hibernian. Roy had struggled to hold down a first-team place and when Hibs freed him, Morton stepped in. Roy was quick to benefit from Erik's experience and coaching prowess. So much so that, by 1972, Roy was just too good for reserve football. When Erik missed a match through illness, Roy replaced him and his form was so good that he was impossible to displace. For Erik at this stage of his career, the time seemed right to concentrate on coaching. Realising goalkeeper was a specialised position, Erik devised routines based on ones his own goalkeeping coach taught him in Denmark as a young man. 'I had always been disappointed in standard of coaching goalkeepers in Scotland, and I thought I could perhaps help other goalies.' Roy Baines himself pays tribute to Erik's talent as a coach.

When I signed for Morton, Erik was well established as first choice. With Hibs I had played under great managers like Bob Shankly and Ernie Turnbull and had played in some big games. One of my first matches for Hibs was against Liverpool in European competition. But Erik taught me everything I know in terms of technique and training methods. He showed me things I had never thought about, like how to fall and where to place your hands on the ball. Working with Erik was the hardest four years of my career. He was the supreme professional and I've never been as fit as when I was working under Erik.

One of Morton's finest ever goalkeepers, Roy Baines himself had a very successful coaching career after he retired from playing. He developed his own coaching methods, which evolved from the great start to his career that Erik gave him.

Erik's last first-team match was a 3–0 victory in November 1972 against Airdrie. He continued to play for the reserves and coach Baines, but eventually gave up playing at the age of 34.

Morton FC in 1966. From left to right, back row: J. Boyd, J. Loughlan, E. Sorensen, F. Nielsen, E. Smith, H. Strachan. Front row: J. Harper, M. Stevenson, B. Gray, A. McGraw, A. McIntyre.

Erik regrets that now, as he feels he had years left in him, but there were extenuating circumstances. Morton had been without a manager since Eric Smith left in 1973. The experienced Jim Townsend had been operating as player-coach but February 1974 found Morton third bottom of the League, in real danger of being relegated. Hal Stewart took the bold step of naming Erik as Morton's manager, with Townsend remaining as player-coach. Erik brought his great professionalism and enthusiasm to the role, and Morton eventually finished a comfortable 14th. It was an encouraging start for Erik, and in April 1974 he made the fortuitous and far-reaching decision to bring Allan McGraw back to the club to look after the youth side. Unfortunately the following season found Morton lacking. The pool of players was not good enough or big enough. They finished a disappointing 17th and failed to qualify for the newly formed Premier League. This led to a parting of the ways for Erik and Morton. It was, needless to say a great disappointment for Erik. 'It was a great honour to be asked to be manager of Morton. It started very well, but I would

49

say a lack of finances and inexperience on my part let us down. It was nevertheless a very exciting time for me.'

After leaving Morton, Erik had short spells in charge of junior sides Largs Thistle and Dalry, where he gave a 16-year-old Jim Leighton his first big break. Erik then concentrated on coaching goalkeepers, becoming a kind of goalies' guru for hire. The list of Scottish goalkeepers that have benefited from Erik's innovative coaching routines is a very long one indeed, with Billy Thomson and Jim Leighton just two who have much to thank Erik for.

I brought the training methods I had learned in Denmark, and I worked with some fine goalies. They weren't always happy because I worked them hard, but they always showed their gratitude afterwards. Even today, Jim Leighton still keeps in touch.

In 1980, Erik returned to management at St Mirren as Ricki McFarlane's assistant, but left when McFarlane was sacked.

Erik then assisted Eddie Morrison during Eddie's short but rewarding stint as Morton manager in 1983, and in late 1983 he again took over as manager of Largs Thistle. His short second spell at Largs demonstrated Erik's tremendous motivational powers.

Erik took over a struggling Largs side that were rooted at the bottom of the Ayrshire Juniors second division with a record of played five, lost five. By the end of the season they were champions having only lost a further two matches. His training routines became the stuff of legend, often going on until after 10 o'clock at night. Largs' Match Secretary, Donald Reid, remembers Erik's tremendous trademark professionalism and enthusiasm.

Erik was a total pro, dedicated to football. He was always immaculately dressed and he insisted the players should ditch the jeans and wear a suit and tie. His whole life was football, and he achieved such a lot at Largs in a short space of time. There was never a dull moment. I remember a match when our goalie had to go off injured and one of our forwards went in goal as a replacement and played well. Erik played him in goal the next game! This was the same player that Erik put on as sub in

another match and then took him off after a minute and a half because Erik said he
wasn't doing what he was told. He really was an amazing bloke!

Erik left Largs and indeed Scotland in 1984 to return to Denmark to take up a job with the railways, and to extend his business interests. He has also coached several Danish sides, including Odense where it all began for him. Incredibly, he still plays football in his mid-60s, although these days outfield, rather than the position that made his name. He has returned periodically over the years to a town that he still holds in great regard, most recently in 2005. His affection for Morton and the Greenock area remains undiminished, and his memories clear. For those of us who say that the summers of our childhood really did last all summer long, then Erik's memories of pre-season training with Morton will strike a chord, and perhaps queries Greenock's reputation as the rain capital of Scotland. 'One of my most vivid memories of Greenock is pre-season training, which always seemed to be during a heatwave. It was just too hot!'

Morton goalkeeper Roy Baines is put through his paces by former Morton goalkeeper Erik Sorensen in a special morning training session for Roy, 1974.

Erik would like to be remembered as an innovative goalkeeper in the fine tradition of Cappielow custodians.

I think people saw that the game could be played in a different way. I hope they saw that I brought a fresh approach and always gave my best. Morton had a fine reputation for goalkeepers. You only need to think of Jimmy Cowan. I like to think I always conducted myself in a good way, in a manner befitting Jimmy Cowan. I think the fans responded to me. I was always given a good reception wherever I went, and the Morton fans were great to me. I loved my time at Cappielow.

Morton playing statistics: (League, League Cup, Scottish Cup)

Season	Appearances
1963–64	5
1964–65	43
1965–66	39
1966–67	46
1970–71	30
1971–72	42
1972–73	11

A Morton Danish Select XI

How is this for a Morton side composed entirely of Danes who played for Morton during the original Scandinavian invasion in 4-3-3 formation? (With a bit of artistic licence to include Lief Holten who only played once and was not that good.) Erik Sorensen; Borge Thorup, John Madsen, Flemming Nielsen, Kaj Johansen; Preben Arentoft, Jorn Sorensen, Bjarne Jensen; Lief Holten, Carl Bertlesen, Per Bartram.

Chapter 4

Joe Mason
An All-Action Player

One of the hardest things in football is for a player to come to a new club and replace a fans' favourite. When that particular favourite is a hero like Allan McGraw then the task becomes nigh impossible. That was the daunting task facing Joe Mason when he joined Morton in 1966 from Kilmarnock. Allan was still a Morton player when Joe joined the club and the two teamed up briefly in a couple of friendly matches before McGraw moved on. The Morton fans' disappointment at losing the talismanic McGraw was soon tempered as Joe plundered 43 League and Cup goals in his first season in a Morton jersey. His goalscoring exploits, skill, agility, enthusiasm and work ethic made Joe a personality player in Hal Stewart's fondly remembered sides of the latter half of the 1960s.

Joe Mason was born in Kilmarnock in 1940 and was brought up in the Townholm area of the town. Times were hard during the war years, and one of the few respites was football. Like so many others Joe learned his football in the streets, along with his brother Alex. He played for his school team and local side Dreghorn Juniors. His displays led to Joe signing for Ayrshire Junior side Lugar Boswell in 1959, joining brother Alex. Ayrshire Juniors was a hard learning ground for a young footballer – even more so than now. 'I learned how to look after myself with Lugar. The juniors were full of hard men and if you didn't stand up for yourself, if you were a bit soft and didn't hold your end up, they would kick you off the park. So I had to learn fast.' Even as a young man, Joe was no shrinking violet. He had left school before he was 15 and became a miner. He worked down the pits for three years, combining the hard shifts with his football.

I would have went anywhere for a game. I worked long shifts down the pits, but me and my mate would play before our shift and after it. I left school at 14½ and went straight down the pit. It wasn't a particularly exciting feeling going down into the blackness in that lift. It was actually quite terrifying to tell you the truth.

At this stage of his career Joe was an inside-forward and his hard-working displays led to a trial for Leicester City in 1960. He impressed Leicester manager Matt Gillies and was offered signing terms.

I was offered £1,000 to sign and my dad was to get £500. Well, my dad had never seen £500 in his life, but I asked for time to think about it. When I went home there was a letter waiting for me from Kilmarnock. I was to go to Rugby Park and meet with Killie manager Willie Waddell. I remember going down to Rugby Park and my dad got a wee half and I signed for nothing. I didn't even know what my wages would be, I was just happy to sign for Kilmarnock. I was a Killie supporter as a boy, and my dad was a supporter all his days and took me regularly. I admired the likes of Willie Toner and Frank Beattie, and it was Frank who helped me settle in.

Joe had joined an excellent Kilmarnock side seemingly destined to be the perennial bridesmaids in the hunt for major honours. They had just lost the 1960 Cup Final to Rangers and had finished runners-up in the League as well. In Joe's five seasons with the club they finished in second place twice, before finally winning the League in season 1964–65. Consequently, with all the talent at Rugby Park, Joe found it hard to secure a regular first-team place.

As an inside-forward, I was competing against the likes of Jackie McInally and Bertie Black, and it was hard to keep them out of the team for any length at a time.

Joe Mason in typical goalmouth action against Motherwell in 1967. He tries to shoot, in a move which led to the second goal.

I couldn't complain too much and did well when called upon. I was Kilmarnock born and bred, and to play for them was a great thing for me.

Joe's record of 27 goals in 56 games at Killie shows that he was a valuable first-team pool player, however, and his record of a goal every two games is testament of his value to them. A League championship medal at last came his way in 1965 when Killie won the League on the last day of the season against Hearts at Tynecastle. It was due reward for years of hard work and near misses by Kilmarnock, but the Killie fans and players were stunned when the architect of the club's success, Willie Waddell, resigned shortly afterwards. 'Willie Waddell was a hard man, probably the hardest I ever came across in football, but he was great for me. He looked after me and always encouraged me. I learned so much from him.'

Joe and Willie Waddell were destined to team up again years later, but in 1966 his Kilmarnock career started to go downhill. 'Malcolm MacDonald took over from Willie Waddell and it's fair to say that we didn't exactly see eye to eye.' The arrival of a new manager did not result in Joe increasing his first-team appearances, but in one of his all-too-rare starts the catalyst for his transfer to Morton occurred. Morton scored a goal with 10 minutes to go and MacDonald blamed Joe. 'After the match MacDonald told me that I'd never play for Kilmarnock again.'

MacDonald was true to his word and Joe never played for Kilmarnock again. He was made available for £2,500. Hal Stewart was all too aware that Allan McGraw felt that his time at Cappielow was drawing to a close and that Allan was keen to move on. Hal was also equally aware that although Allan was not quite the force he had been, the Morton fans would not take kindly to the loss of their talismanic goalscorer, unless he could replace him with an equally flamboyant player. Joe fitted the bill and when he heard he was available Hal made his move.

Joe featured on a collector's card.

Joe was not too hard to deal with and he became a Morton player in July 1966, with Craig Watson going to Killie. The signing terms offered to Joe were a slight improvement on his Kilmarnock ones. 'Hal Stewart offered me 400 cigarettes to sign for Morton! I couldn't believe it. I thought he was joking!' Joe politely declined the offer, but was quite happy to join Morton. Joe and Allan McGraw briefly teamed up on a Scandinavian tour, but when they returned to Scotland Allan was free to go and he joined Hibernian. One can only dream about a partnership of a fully fit McGraw and the hungry and eager Joe Mason. As it was on the only two occasions that they played together Joe scored five times. Joe had joined a Morton side that had just been relegated from the old first division. The highs of the record-breaking 1963–64 side were now a memory and only John Boyd, Morris Stevenson and Hugh

Strachan, a boyhood pal of Joe's, were left at the club. Hal Stewart had set about building a new team, and one that he publicly declared would be better equipped for the top division. Joe's signing had coincided with the appointment of Eric Smith as full-time coach.

Eric had played for Celtic and Leeds under Don Revie. He was a hard, wee man who liked to get you working and get you fit. We started pre-season with punishing stints on Salcoats beach. This was years before Jock Wallace took Rangers to Gullane.

Joe had played most of his career as an inside-forward, but was immediately switched to centre-forward. He soon made the position his own with his trademark enthusiasm and hard work. It was this inherent work ethic allied to his natural goalscoring ability that made him such a hit with the Morton fans.

Joe pictured in training on a programme from 1971.

After what had happened to me at Killie, I was determined to do well at Morton. The fans seemed to sense this, and I immediately struck up a great relationship with them. I like to think I always gave 100 percent and the Morton fans appreciated this. Fans will rarely boo a trier. They'll accept it if you're having a bad game.*

There were not too many bad games for Joe in that first memorable season and he finished the top scorer in Britain with 43 goals. Morton fans' first sight of him was in a friendly at Cappielow against Israeli side Maccabi; Joe scoring from a Joe Harper cross. Joe never looked back, scoring nine times in six League Cup sectional matches as 'Ton qualified to play Aberdeen in the quarter-finals. The first leg at Cappielow brought back memories of the giant-killing 1963–64 season when Morton knocked out higher League opposition in the quarter-final and semi-final. Aberdeen were comprehensively beaten 3–1 in the first leg, but Morton being Morton they managed to lose the return leg 3–0 and tumbled out of the competition. The *Greenock Telegraph* reported that Aberdeen, realising Joe's importance, had him well shackled, but Joe had worked 'like five men' and was of the opinion that it was a miracle he was still standing at the final whistle.

The League, however, was the priority and again memories of the record-breaking League run of 1963–64 were stirred as Morton crushed all comers. All the hard work under Eric Smith paid dividends as Morton won 33 out of 38 games, losing only once and scoring 118 goals. Their points total of 69 was a record at the time. Joe's partnership with the teenage Joe Harper was lethal with 74 goals between them in League and Cup matches. What kind of goals did Joe score? All kinds: tap ins, headers, 25-yard rockets, spectacular overhead efforts. Joe scored his fair share of doubles and hat-tricks that season but there were also several vital single goals that proved to be match winners, like the one against East Fife at Cappielow in December 1966 that secured a vital 2–1 victory.

It had been a memorable first season for Joe, and Morton returned to the top division determined to establish themselves as one of the top sides in the country. Ironically, Morton's first match of the 1967–68 season was against Kilmarnock at Rugby Park in a match Joe was determined to do well in. Unfortunately for Morton, Killie won 3–1 in a match that saw televised highlights that evening. Joe and Morton gained a measure of revenge soon afterwards, however, as the two sides were drawn against each other in the League Cup quarter-final. 'Ton had stormed through their section, winning all six matches and scoring 19 goals. Joe Harper had departed for Huddersfield, but Joe's new striking partner, the Dane Per Bartram, scored 11 of those 19 goals. Confidence was high for the first leg at Cappielow. But that confidence looked misplaced as Killie quickly took a 2–0 lead, but Joe put Morton back in the game with an audacious chip over the Killie 'keeper. Prior to kick-off, Hal Stewart had promised that Morton would go for it and appealed for the fans to get behind the team. The crowd of 10,000 did just that and roared the side

Martin, Rangers' goalkeeper, grabs the ball as Joe Mason tries to connect with a cross by Allan .

on to victory. Willie Allan equalised and Joe set up Bartram for the winning goal of a pulsating match. For the return leg two weeks later, 18 supporters' buses and scores of cars made their way to Ayrshire and another large crowd saw Hal's latest heroes come of age as they won 2–1 on the night and 5–3 on aggregate. Hal Stewart's latest innovation – a 'canary' yellow jersey that gave off a luminous hue under floodlights – only seemed to emphasise Morton's confidence and superiority. Revenge was sweet for Joe as he scored the decisive second goal with a 25-yard pile-driver. It was a tremendous feat for a Morton side just out of the Second Division against a Kilmarnock side containing several members of their championship-winning side and managed by Joe's nemesis Malcolm MacDonald.

The semi-final draw, however, did Morton no favours as they were drawn against a rampant Celtic side fresh from their European Cup triumph in Lisbon only months before. It was lambs to the slaughter as Celtic hammered a shell-shocked

Joe rolls the ball casually into the net for yet another goal against Clyde in 1968.

Morton 7–1 at Hampden with even Jim Craig scoring twice from full-back. One consolation for the 'Ton faithful was Morton's goal – the best of the match – a 25-yard screamer from Preben Arentoft.

Joe remembers the match ruefully but philosophically. 'Oh, we got a doing all right. We did go into the game hoping to surprise them, but it was a juggernaut. They were a fantastic side, but wee Preben still scored the best goal.' Before the end of the season Morton would be back at Hampden twice more, but fate was no kinder to them on both occasions.

After the Celtic game – rather like Celtic or Rangers being knocked out of Europe and then taking it out on some poor, unsuspecting native opposition – Morton took their disappointment out on Airdrie and Stirling Albion, hammering them 4–0 and 6–0 in quick succession. Typically inconsistent, they then went out and lost their next home game against St Johnstone. Their League form was

Joe scores against Airdrie at snowbound Cappielow in 1968.

generally good, however, and they were rarely out of the top half of the table all season. The good form in the League carried over to the Scottish Cup and victories over Falkirk, East Fife and Elgin took Morton into the semi-final against Hearts. With both the Old Firm eliminated, there was never a better chance for a small club like Morton to win the Cup. The first match against Hearts was a nervy, disappointing match that ended 1–1, with Stan Rankin scoring a rare goal. The replay was a better match, with Morton scoring an early goal through Willie Allan. Hearts equalised through George Miller in the 33rd minute and the tie went into extra-time. With only minutes left Hearts winger Jensen ran through the Morton defence only to be upended by 'keeper Bobby Russell. The penalty was converted and Morton were out, disappointingly to a Hearts side nowhere near as good as Morton. 'We really should have beaten Hearts. We just didn't perform to our abilities in both matches. It was certainly one of the biggest disappointments of my career.'

The season did end on a high for Joe and Morton as a late run of victories guaranteed them sixth place in the League and a place in the following season's Inter Cities Fairs Cup. Revenge of sorts was gained against Hearts in the final League match. A 1–0 victory, courtesy of a 25-yarder from Joe, ensured qualification for Europe. The *Greenock Telegraph* called the goal 'Morton's £220 goal' as that was the amount paid by the pools company for sixth place. The goal against Hearts ensured that Joe again finished the season as Morton's top goalscorer with 23 goals.

Morton were drawn against Chelsea in the Fairs Cities Cup in September 1968. The tie against Chelsea coincided with Morton's worst run of form for several seasons. The League Cup, normally a tournament the club did well in, had proved disastrous, with all six sectional matches against Celtic, Rangers and Partick Thistle being lost. Only two goals had been scored and 19 conceded. They had managed one solitary victory in the League when they travelled down to London to meet the might of Chelsea. Despite a spirited first-half performance, 'Ton were hammered 5–0. They acquitted themselves much better in the return at Cappielow, losing 4–3 in a pulsating match. This encouraging performance proved to be the boost that Morton needed and their season ended in a top-10 spot and another semi-final appearance against Celtic in the Scottish Cup. Once more, however, 'Ton found themselves on the wrong end of a heavy defeat, losing 4–1 despite taking the lead in the second minute. The scoreline flattered Celtic somewhat, as Morton had performed well on the day.

Revenge was gained the following month, when Morton memorably inflicted a 4–2 victory over Celtic at Parkhead, with Per Bartram scoring a hat-trick in seven minutes. At this stage of his career Joe was happy to take a back seat to the hot new striking partnership of 'Batman and Robin' (Bartram and Harper). Joe would now occasionally play in a more withdrawn role, where his subtle promptings from midfield provided numerous goalscoring opportunities for his colleagues. But Morton being Morton, and every player having his price, both Harper and Bartram were moved on before the decade was over.

The transfer comings and goings at Cappielow could be truly mind-boggling at times. In just a few short months Harper, Bartram, Preben Arentoft, Morris Stevenson, Willie Allan and Barney Jensen left the club. Joe saw a virtual assembly line of strikers coming in, such as Pat Ferry, and the inimitable Billy 'Sugar' Osborne. Osborne proved a great fans' favourite with his powerful and unorthodox style, and served the club well for over six seasons after joining from Dunoon Juniors. Joe would sporadically still appear as striker, but for the remainder of his career at Cappielow he played in his now favoured role of midfield 'schemer'. He was greatly helped in that regard with the arrival of the famous Bobby Collins in 1969. Then aged 38, Collins, 'The Wee Barra', was a hard little pro who had seen and done it all in a 20-year career with Celtic, Everton, Leeds and Scotland.

Playing and training with guys like Bobby Collins and Gerry Sweeney was a big thing for me. They were big believers in you played like you trained and it rubbed off on me. In training I always tried to match the effort they put in and when I saw how little Bobby Collins could dominate a game...I mean, he was only about five feet four, I thought that's what I want to do.

Joe certainly put the effort in both on and off the field. His all-action style reflected his fiery temperament. He was ordered off five times in his career and, like Denis Law, whose style of play Joe resembled, he liked to get his retaliation in first. In fact, after his fifth ordering off, Joe was invited up to the Scottish Football Association offices for a meeting with 'the beaks'. He was informed that one more ordering off could result in a *sine die* ban. 'That warning was a lesson for me and I heeded it – I was never sent off again. I just didn't like dirty big centre-halves kicking me and, if they did, I made sure I kicked them back.'

Indeed he did, and he did not just kick the offending defenders. In a match at Cappielow against Dunfermline in 1969, Joe had been kicked up and down the park from the first whistle by Pars' stopper Roy Barry. A strategically placed elbow left Barry lying on the turf but, unfortunately for Joe, a linesman had caught him in the act and he was ordered off. Two minutes later 'Ton were down to nine men when Barney Jensen also reacted to some tough treatment and retaliated. The big Dane left the field in tears.

Joe was a big admirer of the Danish players at Cappielow. 'I thought they were smashing lads – great trainers, dedicated professionals and good players. Erik Sorensen was a top class goalie, wee Preben Arentoft was a tremendous worker and big Per Bartram could really stick the ball away.'

So, if Joe was an awkward customer to play against, what was he like as a teammate? Joe's old friend and teammate Hugh Strachan good-naturedly remembers Joe as:

A crabbit sod! If things weren't going well the dressing room could be pretty interesting at half-time. I remember in one game, I won the ball in a tackle, strolled out of defence like Beckenbauer, and flighted what I thought was a perfectly-weighted cross-field pass to Joe standing near the touchline. The ball flew over his head and he started after it but soon gave up as the ball ran on for miles. He turned round, gestured at me and shouted, 'dae ye think I've got ******* wings?'

Hugh Strachan was a tremendously consistent defender who hardly missed a match in five seasons. He played in the 1963 League Cup Final and was a reliable presence in the Morton defence. He recalls the circumstances of his departure from Cappielow in 1969.

I had been with Morton for six years and was due a benefit. One day Hal called me into his office and I thought, 'Oh this will be about the money I'm due.' Hal says to me, 'I'm going to have to let you go, Hughie.' He gave me some excuse about freeing up some money with my wages, but I knew it was just so he didn't have to pay the benefit. I walked out the office and met one of the young players and he said, 'I hear one of the big names is getting a free transfer.' I said, 'Aye it's ******* me!'

Hugh had the last laugh on Hal. He moved to his home-town side Kilmarnock and played for them in Europe. When Killie freed him as well he moved to Partick Thistle where he had a real Indian summer. Aged 33, he was a member of the Partick Thistle side who thrashed Celtic in the 1972 League Cup Final, earning a winners' medal almost a decade after his Final with Morton. He then played in Europe with Thistle and demonstrated his trademark consistency over three seasons, rarely missing a match. Rarely can a player who was given three free transfers have had such a distinguished and rewarding end to his career than the self-effacing Strachan.

Morton with the Renfrewshire Cup in 1967. Joe Mason is seated, third from right.

Gerry Sweeney was a teammate of Joe Mason for five years and remembers him with great affection.

Oh Joe, Joe. What a guy. It was never dull when Joe was around. His patter was great and he would kid around when the time was right. But above all, he was a great professional. He had a good touch, was a good reader of the game and was very consistent, but above all he was a hard worker who could always be relied on to score goals.

Arthur Montford remembers Joe for his 'quick darting runs'. Arthur says about Joe:

In a strange way Joe reminded me of the great Jimmy Mason of Third Lanark. Both were quite slight in stature, but Joe in particular could be quite aggressive.

Both were very adept at running through with his fellow striker and pouncing on a chance.

Joe Harper formed a short-lived but lethal partnership with Joe and remembers their friendly rivalry and Joe's generous nature.

Joe Mason was one of the guys at Morton who helped me a lot. We scored goals galore when we played together and part of that was a competitive thing. We wanted to help each other, but we also wanted to score more goals than each other. Joe was also a very intelligent player. He played with his head and was very clever on the ball. All in all, a big influence on my career.

Although there had been some interest from other clubs over the years, including Newcastle, Joe remained happy at Cappielow, a senior and much-respected pro. He had begun to coach the young players at the club, and at 32 was still very much a regular in the first team.

In October 1972, Morton played Rangers in a League match at Ibrox. Despite winning the European Cup-winners' Cup only months before, Rangers were going through one of their periodic crises. The match was notable for the debut to much fanfare of Quentin Young. But it was Joe who stole Young's thunder with a sublime performance. Joe ran the match from midfield as Morton played Rangers off the pitch. Their superiority was not matched by the final score of 1–1, with Don Gillies scoring Morton's goal. The biggest surprise of the day, however, was reserved for Joe.

I had got changed after the match and was leaving the away dressing room. Tommy McLean, who I knew from my Kilmarnock days, was waiting outside the dressing room. He called me over and handed me a piece of paper. There was a phone number written on it and Tommy told me I was to phone the number that night. When I rang the number the voice at the other end said, 'Hello Joe, it's Willie Waddell here, you'll be coming up to sign for Rangers on Monday morning.' I was gobsmacked. I went up to Ibrox on the Monday and signed without any fuss at all. I had a great six years at Cappielow, but I couldn't turn down the chance to sign for one of the biggest clubs in the world.

The fee involved was a modest £10,000, and technically Joe had been 'tapped' by Rangers, but it is almost certain that the wily Hal Stewart knew everything that was going on. Joe was 32, and it was a dream move at that stage of his career. Informed opinion was that he was being signed not so much for his playing abilities, as for an eventual job on the coaching staff. And that was how it transpired. Joe played only 18 games for Rangers before being asked to join the coaching staff at the start of the 1973–74 season. A short time afterwards, Joe had indeed retired as a player, and was named reserve-team coach. 'Waddell told me he was going to teach me how to be a coach and he was a great man to learn from. Why he signed me at that stage of my career I'll never know, but perhaps he saw something in me all those years ago at Kilmarnock.'

Joe struck up a good relationship with manager Jock Wallace and coached the reserves for several successful seasons. After Wallace left for Leicester, John Greig took over and Joe eventually became Greig's assistant. It was not a happy partnership, as Joe and Greig frequently disagreed over training and tactics. Eventually, Joe's time at Ibrox was to end abruptly and disappointingly in 1983.

When Jock Wallace left Rangers for Leicester in 1978, he asked me to join him as his assistant. I had to turn him down as my wife's parents were both ill and we didn't want to leave them. When Jock came back in 1983, I was called into a meeting with the Chairman, Rae Simpson, and was told that Jock wanted me to resign.

Joe had been unceremoniously sacked. Rangers were in turmoil at the time and it looked as if Wallace wanted a fresh start with his own men, but the suspicion lingered that Wallace had resented Joe turning down the move to Leicester. 'These things happen in football. I'll never say a bad word about my time at Rangers, or indeed at Morton and Kilmarnock, but that experience soured me for football, and I've never been back in the game since, even though I was offered several jobs.'

After 25 years in the game, Joe was unemployed and looking for a new career. He found it in the shape of a bakery business in Kilmarnock, which he still runs today. He is still a keen follower of football, although he does feel that his maxim of 'train hard and play hard' is not always followed by the modern footballer.

I feel as if some footballers today don't realise what a great life it is. Some of them don't want to play two games in a week. And training and coaching wise, well some of the methods leave a lot to be desired. I was watching Barcelona on the television recently and they were playing in little triangles. It's a simple tactic, but it's how all the top sides play. But I was doing that 25 years ago with Rangers, yet I don't see many Scottish sides doing it.

Joe has fond memories of his time with Morton. 'I had a magical time at Morton; it was some of the happiest years of my career. It was a great wee club, the fans were great to me and I would love to see them back in the top League again, maybe against Kilmarnock. But just don't ask me who I would support!'

Morton playing statistics: (League, League Cup, Scottish Cup)

Season	Appearances	Goals
1966–67	47	43
1967–68	42	23
1968–69	36 +2subs	6
1969–70	31 +3subs	12
1970–71	35 +1sub	11
1971–72	42	6
1972–73	12	3

Chapter 5
Gerry Sweeney
Eleven Players in One

It is an old adage in football that you only get out of it what you put in. In Gerry Sweeney's case a professional career of some 600 games over 16 years is a tribute to his remarkable ability, consistency, fitness and above all work rate. In those 16 years, Gerry earned the respect of teammates, opponents and fans alike for his unstinting professionalism and will to win. He remains a fondly remembered figure amongst Morton fans, and when fans and pundits sporadically pick their best ever Morton XI, then Gerry's name often crops up.

Gerry was a man of many positions. He literally was 11 players rolled into one. At one stage it was his versatility and ability to play in a number of positions that threatened to hamper his progress, but he finally settled down with Morton as a driving wing-half or midfielder. Later in his career he became an accomplished right-back at the very top of the English game. For Joe Harper, Gerry is one of Morton's most unsung players.

Gerry was the engine room of the Morton side that I played in during the late '60s. His strengths were his unflagging energy and enthusiasm that allowed him to work all over the park. He also never gave up and even when we were being beaten he would always try and lift the heads. His sense of humour was great and he was always full of fun. A great guy and a great character.

Gerry Sweeney was born in Renfrew in 1945, at the tail end of the war. Gerry was the youngest of seven brothers, all of whom were football daft from an early age. In fact, there were so many Sweeney brothers that they were able to form their own team, learning their skills on the streets like so many others of the time, and taking part in matches that would last from dawn till dusk. The young Gerry played for his school and the Boys Guild before joining Glentyan Thistle, the juvenile side who through the years has provided Morton with such talents as Tommy Turner and Jim Hunter. As a teenager Gerry played mainly as an inside-left, or twin striker, where he liked to feed off the old-fashioned bustling centre-forwards.

Glentyan hailed from Johnstone just outside Paisley and, when he was 16, Gerry signed for junior outfit Johnstone Burgh who were then beginning to establish themselves as one of the top junior sides in the country. Gerry quickly made his mark at that level, scoring regularly, and he began to attract the attention of some top senior sides.

I was a bit younger than most junior players of the time and I was that wee bit weaker physically. But in the juniors they took no prisoners; age was no barrier. I took some tough punishment, but it toughened me up for pro football.

In 1964, Gerry was invited for a week's trial with Leicester City, but before anything could happen, Celtic stepped in. 'Jimmy McGrory was the manager, and I had been a bit of a Celtic fan when I was younger, so it was a dream come true when I signed for them.'

Gerry joined a Celtic side at a pivotal time in their history. The club had been in decline for a number of years and Rangers were dominant. Radical action was required and not long after Gerry joined the club, Jock Stein replaced the gentlemanly McGrory. As a young reserve Gerry did not initially have too much contact with Stein, but remembers the odd rollicking from him, as well as the occasional pat on the back. Gerry combined his football with an engineering apprenticeship.

He was part-time with Celtic, training two nights a week plus a Sunday, and was a regular in the reserves. First-team opportunities were limited, however, as Stein set about restructuring the club. Not long after Gerry joined Celtic they won the Scottish Cup and it was obvious to him that something special was about to happen.

Under Stein, there was a great atmosphere and he turned the whole club around. The era of the 'quality street kids' was just around the corner, and things were beginning to happen just I left. McGrain, Macari and Dalglish all came through not long afterwards.

Gerry was given a free transfer in July 1966 and was reinstated to the juniors, signing for Renfrew. There it was blatantly obvious he was too good for that level and after only a few months Morton came calling. Gerry became a Morton player in November 1966. Gerry credits former Celtic player Jim Kennedy as a big factor in Morton's interest.

Jim Kennedy was the Morton left-back and skipper in 1966, but crucially he had been at Celtic Park for a season with Gerry. Jim had indeed primed Gerry that Morton would be a good move for him.

I have a feeling that big Jim Kennedy might have had an influence on Morton coming in for me. Jim thought I had a good chance of first-team football with

Morton. Morton had me watched in a match for Renfrew in which I scored four goals and a few weeks later I signed for them.

Gerry had joined a Morton side riding high in the old Second Division. They had all but guaranteed promotion and were winning match after match. So initially it looked as if Gerry would struggle to get a game. But a few weeks after signing, Gerry was handed his debut against Raith Rovers at Kirkcaldy at inside-left, acquitted himself well and played another dozen games until the end of the season, scoring three goals.

'Ton clinched the championship in April 1967 with a 5–0 win over Stranraer at Cappielow. On the same day that 100–1 shot Foinavon won the Grand National, Gerry scored twice, including Morton's 100th League goal of the season and he was hoisted on his teammates' shoulders at the end of the match.

It was fantastic to be part of all that so soon after joining the club and I settled in quite quickly. We had a great bunch of lads. Guys who knew the game, like Hugh Strachan, who was a great help to the younger boys. When Hughie moved on, big Billy Gray took over that role. There was the great enthusiast Joe Mason, who you could always rely on to score goals. Then wee Joe Harper came back from England. Joe was our very own Gerd Muller, with that low centre of gravity. It was fun on and off the park. And of course the Danish players were so dedicated in their outlook on the game. There was a lot of schoolboy pranks, all the laughs off the pitch made it for me. But we knew when to stop the carry on and concentrate on the football. There was never any trouble, no fights or arguments. And Hal [Stewart] was just fantastic. The first time I saw Minder *and Arthur Daly, I just thought of Hal.*

Gerry's first full season at Cappielow, season 1967–68, was one of the most exciting but ultimately disappointing in the club's history.

A top-six finish guaranteed European football the following season, but there were semi-final defeats in both Cup competitions, against Celtic in the League Cup and disappointingly Hearts in the Scottish Cup. Some consolation was gained with Morton winning the Scottish National five-a-side competition. This televised event

Gerry with two other young
hopefuls in the Cappielow
dressing room in 1966.

from the Kelvin Hall was immensely popular and 2,000 fans witnessed Morton winning the trophy in April 1968. They scored 15 goals in the process with Gerry top scorer with seven. The Morton five were: Gerry, goalie Bobby Russell, Billy Gray, Preben Arentoft and Willie Allan. Morton then competed in the British five-a-side championship with less success, being eliminated in the first round. A year later Morton successfully defended their Scottish trophy, beating Hibs 2–0 in the Final. Paisley Ice Rink housed 4,000 fans, with Gerry and Joe Harper scoring. Morton's winning side this time was: Leif Neilsen, Gerry, Gray, Allan, Harper and Per Bartram. These were heady days at Cappielow and a time that Gerry recalls with great fondness.

One of the highlights of my time at Cappielow was our Fairs Cup matches in 1968. We were looking for some glamorous foreign opposition, but of course drew Chelsea, who to be fair had some great players like Peter Osgood and Charlie Cooke. We got a real hammering at Stamford Bridge, but the return was one hell of a night. We went out really determined to do well, and at one stage we were 3–1 up and the crowd were going ballistic. Chelsea were panicking like hell, and then Billy Gray smacked the crossbar, and they went up the park and scored. That was a real sickener and we eventually lost 4–3 on the night, but it was a fantastic night.

Another Scottish Cup semi-final ended in disappointment the following season when 'Ton fell to Celtic. The final result of 4–1 to Celtic flattered them somewhat as Morton had played very well. They had even opened the scoring in the second minute when Gerry, playing on the left, set up Willie Allan. 'We had a real chance in that game, but we gave away a couple of careless goals before half-time, and then one early in the second half and that killed us. But a few weeks later we showed just what we could do against them.'

The story of Morton's 4–2 defeat of Celtic at Parkhead and Per Bartram's seven-minute hat-trick on 28 April 1969 has been told many times, but for Gerry it was particularly satisfying.

Celtic had just won the treble and had paraded their trophies just before the kick-

off. We were meant to be lambs to the slaughter, but perhaps they were resting on their laurels, and we just gave them a doing. Big Per [Bartram] was on fire. I remember big Billy McNeil shouting at me about Per's elbows. Per was that type of bustling centre-forward and he really enjoyed himself that night.

The line-ups for the successive Scottish Cup semi-final matches give a measure of the comings and goings at Cappielow. Of the 12 that played in the Hearts ties in 1968, only five started against Celtic the following year. Bobby Russell, John Loughlin, Jim Kennedy, Preben Arentoft, Morris Stevenson and Tony Taylor all left the club in the space of a few months. As Gerry says:

An intricate training routine. Gerry with Byarne Jensen, Per Bastram and Morris Stevenson, 1968.

Well, Morton survived by selling. It was as simple as that. It would have been nice to have kept some of the players, and keep the side together a bit longer – but it wasn't a well-off club. It was frustrating at times because just when it looked like we were building a good side, someone would be sold. A lot of promises were made, but never followed through.

By this stage in his career Gerry was beginning to prove his versatility. His early Morton career had seen him play as a left-winger and an inside-left (really a left-sided midfielder), but he was equally adept with his right foot, and was soon being switched about all over the field. For a spell he replaced the man who recommended him to Morton, Jim Kennedy, at left-back before he was switched to right-back.

Tony Taylor had been with Celtic with me, and he signed for Morton not long after me. We were good mates and in training we were always testing each other. He was great at going past his man, and I would tell him that if I was a full-back he would

Gerry and his Morton teammates are congratulated by Hal Stewart on winning the Second Division championship in 1967.

never get by me. We were short of defenders for one game, and I was switched to left-back. I felt comfortable there immediately and it was the same in other positions.

And so a pattern began to emerge that wherever there was a need, Gerry would plug the gap. For example, in his first match at left-back, he was switched to right-back after 20 minutes when John Loughlin was injured. When Gerry first joined Morton, the terms 'wing-half' and 'inside-forward' were beginning to be phased out. Most Scottish sides still played a basic 4-2-4 formation, usually with two wingers and two strikers. In the days before Sky television, with players numbered from 1 to 100, the number on the jersey more or less corresponded with the position the

Gerry is hoisted aloft aftewr scoring twice against Stranraer as Morton clinched the title. Left to right: H. Strachan, J. Lough, Gerry, J. Kennedy, P. Bartram, M. Stevenson, I. Anderson, J. Mason.

player occupied. It may not be strictly true that Gerry played in every position for Morton, but he certainly wore just about every number on his jersey. In one game against Kilmarnock in 1970 he even took over in goal from the injured Leif Neilsen and did not acquit himself too badly. But it was as a full-back that Gerry won his biggest honour in his career when he was picked to represent the Scottish League against the Irish League in December 1969.

I was sitting in the house and my brother was reading the evening paper. He said that the Scottish League pool had been named and he read out the names. When he read out mine, I thought he was joking and told him to get lost. It was only when he showed me the paper that I actually began to believe it. I think I was picked as much for my performances against Celtic as anything else. I had been directly up against Jimmy Johnstone a couple of times and I had done well, and we had some good results against them. What stands out as much as anything about the whole experience was when we had all met up at the team's hotel. I could be quite loud in my own environment, but here I was, wee Gerry Sweeney from the Morton with all these internationals from Celtic and Rangers and the like, and I was a bit intimidated. I was holding back a wee bit. And big John Greig, who was the captain of course, must have noticed this and he made a big show of involving me and bringing me into the group. Willie Johnston was there, and he was the object of some story, and big Greigy shouts me over, saying something like, 'Hey Gerry, come over here and listen to this. What do you make o' this wee so and so?' And of course I joined them, and they made me the focus of the conversation. I thought it was a great gesture, a captain's gesture if you like, and I really appreciated it. And it put me at my ease, and I felt part of the group.

As for the game itself, Gerry acquitted himself well at right-back in a 5–2 victory, with his recently departed teammate Joe Harper helping himself to a double. 'It was a fantastic experience. Hal told me he was really proud of me. I've still got the jersey. It holds pride of place in my house. My only regret is that it didn't happen often enough.'

As a new decade dawned, Gerry's development as a footballer and leader was

The Morton squad in 1968. Back row, left to right: T. Taylor, G. Sweeney, B. Jensen, D. Laughton, B. Russell, S. Rankin, P. Bartram, B. Thorup, J. Mason, B. Gray, E. Smith. Front row: P. Arentoft, J. Kerr, J. Loughlan, G. Douglas, M. Stevenson, H. Strachan, W. Allen, J. Ward.

recognised when he was installed as Morton captain. His first real test in that role came in the newly formed Texaco Cup, which pitted Scottish and English sides who had not qualified for European football against each other. Gerry seemed to relish these games against English opposition and Morton's four matches in 1970 in the Texaco Cup saw some of Gerry's finest games for the club. Gerry had also by now found a regular position in midfield, linking the defence and attack. The home tie in the first round against West Bromwich Albion will long be remembered as one of Morton's finest hours, as they recovered from an early Stan Rankin own goal to defeat their more fancied opponents 2–1 with two goals from Billy Osborne. There was some debate over Billy's second goal and initially the referee did not give it – until Gerry chased the linesman to the halfway line that is!

Gerry had picked up an injury after only three minutes, but shook it off to give an outstanding performance. The crowd of 10,000 fans gave Morton a standing ovation at the end of the match and Gerry was acclaimed as 'Morton's hero' by Hal Stewart after the match. The Birmingham newspapers wrote the one-goal deficit off as a minor irritation, comparing Morton's victory to 'a Rolls Royce being overtaken by a motor scooter'. The victory was no fluke, however, and just to prove it 'Ton won again in the second leg at The Hawthorns with 'Sugar' Osborne scoring the only goal. As good as Gerry was over the two matches, it was surely big, bustling Billy

Osborne's finest hour in a Morton jersey. These victories were a tremendous boost for Scottish football against a West Brom side that had won the FA Cup the two years before and included Asa Hartford, Tony Brown and Jeff Astle. The games were won and lost in midfield with Gerry and Bobby Collins completely dominating.

Unfortunately, Morton could not carry on their fine run of form in the first leg of the next round against Wolves. The 'Ton defence could not handle the aerial prowess of Irish centre-forward Derek Dougan and the wing play of David Wagstaffe, and the home tie ended in a 3–0 defeat. Pride was restored at Molineux, however, with man-of-the-match Sweeney scoring one and setting up the other as Morton led 2–0 after an hour, and threatened several times to level the tie. Wolves pulled a goal back, however, and the result ended 2–1 to 'Ton, but it was still a famous victory for Morton over one of the top English sides of the time. In retrospect it may well be that it was Gerry's performances in the Texaco ties that sealed his transfer to Bristol City at the end of that season. He had shown that he could live in the company of top-class English sides. Morton finished the 1970–71 season in eighth position, their best placing for four seasons. Unusually, there was no Cup run, but for Gerry it was his most consistent season. He was an ever present, making 46 appearances, and his form and consistency had not gone unnoticed. He had found a permanent role in midfield and by now he was keen to test himself elsewhere.

The Texaco Cup matches gave me a taste for the English game and I let Hal know I was keen to move. There were a couple of offers for me and I could have gone to Leeds United. But I reasoned that if I picked Leeds, it would only be as cover for the likes of Giles and Bremner, and I figured that it would be better a regular for Bristol City than a reserve for Leeds.

Many players would perhaps have picked the safe option and plumped for Leeds and the easy option of picking up a good wage as a fringe player, but Gerry wanted to play first-team football, and he commendably picked Bristol City. He was impressed by City manager Alan Dicks and he felt that the club was going places.

Gerry signed for Bristol City in May 1971 for the bargain fee of £25,000. City at that time were a mid-table side in the old English Second Division. Under the astute Dicks, City were a side on the rise, eventually winning promotion to the First Division in 1976 where they stayed for several seasons.

In 1974, Gerry crossed swords with Joe Jordan, his old teammate at Morton, in the FA Cup. Leeds were League champions and the toughest, most complete side in the country. It was a major shock when City won at Elland Road after a replay with Donnie Gillies, another ex-Morton player, scoring the only goal. The two sides were to clash often when City eventually won promotion to the top League, and Joe starred for Leeds and later Manchester United. Any lasting friendships were put on hold for the duration of the match, as these two ultimate competitors set about each other. As Joe explains:

Whenever we played against each other we would meet as friends after the match, but never before. It was all about focusing on the game. When I first joined Morton, Gerry had been there a couple of years and I actually used to travel down from Glasgow to training with him along with Tommy Coakley and Billy Gray. Gerry was always exceptionally fit and a very good influence on the younger players. He had good pace, was very determined and basically was a winner. His bubbly personality was a great help in the dressing room. Over the course of a season you obviously have your ups and downs, especially at a club like Morton, and Gerry was a very positive influence in that way. You need a Gerry Sweeney type to lift the heads and offer encouragement when things aren't going so well. It was no surprise to me that he went on to have a long and distinguished career at Bristol City.

Indeed he did. Gerry went on to play over 400 games for Bristol City in his 10 years there. He played in midfield initially then established himself as first-choice right-back. He proved to be a very influential player in City's promotion-winning side of 1975–76, scoring several vital goals. He was then a permanent fixture as City achieved unheard of success in the First Division. He was skipper for several seasons and felt he improved immeasurably as a player as he was obviously up against better players.

In Scotland I really enjoyed matching myself against tricky little wingers like Willie Henderson and Jimmy Johnstone. In England, the best winger I came across was John Robertson, who was a different type of winger, a thinking man's winger. I loved playing against him. He was probably the best player that I played against.

The feeling was mutual as Robertson is on record as declaring Gerry as his toughest opponent. Norman Hunter, the former Leeds United legend, had a successful spell at Bristol City after leaving Leeds, and he too was an admirer of Gerry, considering him the best player he ever played with at City. Sadly for Gerry, his career with Bristol City came to a premature and disappointing end when he was one of eight City players forced to accept redundancy when the club went bankrupt.

Well it was financial mismanagement of the highest scale. For the club to get so far and then promise players contracts that they couldn't fulfil, and then blame the players for being greedy, was pretty unbelievable. We had given everything for the club and I think we ended up with a redundancy payment of eight pence in the pound. But the main thing was that the club survived and the fans had a team to support.

At 36, Gerry was still very fit, and signed for York City, but after a season there decided to retire. He teamed up with his old Morton colleague Tommy Coakley and entered management with several non-League sides before the pair had a very successful spell at Walsall, guiding them to promotion to the old Second Division. The emotional attachment to Bristol City was strong, however, and in the mid-1990s Gerry returned to Ashton Gate as a scout and then schoolboy coach. When Joe Jordan became manager of City for a second time, he thought so highly of Gerry that he promoted him as his assistant in 1995. Joe explains Gerry's qualities.

Gerry was and still is very highly thought of in the Bristol area, and he had proved at Walsall that he was an excellent coach, so when we had a wee backroom reshuffle at City, I had no hesitation in bringing him in, and his qualities as a player were

Morton in 1970. Back row, left to right: G. Sweeney, B. Osborne, J. Murray, E. Sorensen, S. Rankin, L. Nielsen, D. Laughton, B. McDerment, J. Mason. Middle row: E. Smith, G. Anderson, E. Hannigan, D. Hayes, G. O'Neil, H. Stewart. Front row: J. Lavelle, J. Brand, M. Hepburn, B. Collins.

just as evident as a coach. He was the ideal foil for me and just the type you would want as your assistant.

Joe was sacked in 1997 and to Gerry's immense pride he became Bristol City manager – for one match only. As a result, Gerry can lay claim to be Bristol City's most successful manager with a 100 percent record – played one, won one. Gerry then left the club and he now works for the Press Association, relaying match-day information, and as a match-day host at the club.

His love of the area and the club is reciprocated by the fans. One only needs to log on to any of the club websites for an example of the regard that he is held in the Bristol area. The City fans have recognised in Gerry the qualities that long ago endeared him to their Morton counterparts. His enthusiasm and commitment, along with his whole-hearted approach to the game, have ensured that Gerry Sweeney has and will be fondly remembered by fans. For Gerry's part he has nothing but great memories of his time at Cappielow. He returned twice to Cappielow as a Bristol City player. The first time in a friendly in 1973 when City won 1–0, with guess who scoring the goal. The second time was in 1979 in an Anglo-Scottish tie. On both occasions he was given a warm welcome by the Cappielow faithful. He is also extremely modest about his abilities saying:

The Morton squad assemble for pre-season training in 1969.

I was a bread-and-butter player. I worked hard on my strengths, which were bags of energy, hard work and winning tackles. Eric Smith used to say that you train the way that you want to play. I agree with that – I always tried to train and play as hard as I could, and it worked for me.

Gerry Sweeney a bread-and-butter player? For once Gerry, the fans may disagree.

Morton playing statistics: (League, League Cup, Scottish Cup)

Season	Appearances	Goals
1966–67	13	3
1967–68	44 +2subs	6
1968–69	43	1
1969–70	38	5
1970–71	42	6

Chapter 6

Davie Hayes
'Hannibal'

Every side needs a battler. He is not perhaps the most skilful player on the planet, but leads by example with an in-built never-say-die spirit. Look up the definition of 'battler' in the dictionary and do not be surprised if Davie Hayes's name is there. The cliché 'if you're good enough, you're old enough' could also be applied to Davie Hayes. Handed his first-team debut for Morton at the age of 16, he took it all in his stride. By 18 he was a first-team regular, and became a much admired and respected player in his 15 seasons at Cappielow, several as skipper. He was a tough and almost feared opponent, and a teammate and leader that could be relied upon in the heat of battle. His slide tackles became the stuff of legend. He played at a time when every side in Scotland had a top winger and Davie's duels with the likes of Davie Cooper, Ian Scanlon, Peter Weir and Eamonn Bannon, to name just a few, would often have a huge bearing on the result of the match. Although he had several short spells with other clubs when his career ended at Cappielow, it is for his 15 years with Morton that Davie is so well remembered.

David Hayes was born in Glasgow in 1953 and he was brought up in the Denniston and Gallowgate areas of the city. There was no particular football background in his family but Davie, like so many others before him, found the streets of Glasgow an ideal proving ground to hone his skills. His early football consisted of schools and youth teams, and it was while playing for Anfield Boys Club that he came to the attention of Morton.

Eric Smith was the Morton coach at the time, and his brother-in-law was a teammate of mine at Anfield Boys Club. Eric must have been watching his brother-in-law and noticed me. I signed for Morton in 1969 when I was 15. They were the first club to ask me and I jumped at the chance. I had always wanted to be a professional footballer. When I was growing up in Glasgow there was always talk about so and so being a great footballer, but that's only half the story. It's what goes with it. The training, the things you have to give up to get there – staying in at night, early to bed, no drinking. It's the hard work behind it that a lot of people don't see. You can have all the skill in the world, but if you don't have the self-discipline and the will to succeed, you won't last.

Davie signed amateur professional forms and initially played with the under-16s, progressing quickly to the under-18s, still aged 15, and was named as a substitute for the Scottish Youth Under-18s. Davie combined full-time training with a job at Baird Brothers, a local Greenock firm, as an apprentice joiner. By the time he turned 16 he was the reserve side's regular right-back, alongside the youthful Joe Jordan. It may surprise those who remember Davie as the quintessential small, stocky, hard-tackling full-back, but at this stage of his career he was a right-sided midfielder or centre-back. Eric Smith spotted his potential, however, and he was quickly moved to right-back.

When I signed for Morton I didn't set myself any goals, like I was going to be in the first team at such and such a stage – it just sort of happened. I worked hard and Eric Smith took to me and taught me a lot. Eric did just about everything. He looked at players, signed players, took training, coached the side. He taught me a lot. He was an excellent coach and he knew his stuff.

In 1970, Morton played in the inaugural Texaco Cup, a British Cup for English and Scottish sides that had failed to qualify for Europe the previous season. After

knocking out West Bromwich Albion in the first round, Morton then lost the second-round home tie 3–0 against Wolverhampton Wanderers. Probably thinking that the tie was lost, Hal Stewart and Eric Smith decided that now was the time to give some of the younger players a chance, and named Davie along with the equally youthful George Anderson in the side for the return leg at Molineux. It could have been viewed as throwing the lambs to the slaughter. Morton, however, had a history of giving young talents their chance at an early age. And Davie was no ordinary talent. Despite his tender years he feared no one on the park, especially his immediate opponent on the night, left-winger David Wagstaffe who had destroyed Morton in the first leg with his pinpoint crossing. Before the kick off Morton's revered midfield general Bobby Collins rather unkindly described Wagstaffe to Davie as having 'the heart of a pea'.

Eric Smith just told me to go out and hit Wagstaffe right away. So first tackle – bang! Second tackle – bang! Third tackle – well, there was no third tackle. Wagstaffe had the ball but I wasn't anywhere near him, but Bobby Collins shouted, 'Hit him wee man!' and Wagstaffe turned around looking for me and lost the ball. I wasn't going out to hurt him, I was just putting in hard tackles, doing my best to win the ball, but letting him know I was there.

With the Wagstaffe threat nullified, Morton, with Bobby Collins dictating the play, won the match 2–1 and could easily have levelled the tie on aggregate. The *Greenock Telegraph* described Davie's inclusion as 'surprising, but effective' and it remains a highlight of Davie's career.

Bobby Collins had a great game that night. He was hitting the ball everywhere – 40-, 50-yard balls – unbelievable. He was a great guy to learn from, a really hard wee man, he was only about five feet three, but brilliant. He was coaching us at that time as well and he looked after the young boys on and off the field. I remember another game against Rangers at Ibrox when we won 2–0 and he scored. He smashed the ball into an open goal from about a yard out. He loved that!

The game Davie refers to was in 1970 when Morton, with their three young talents – Hayes (16), Joe Jordan (18) and George Anderson (16) – very much to the fore, humbled Rangers in their own backyard. The future looked bright for Morton with young talent like that breaking through, but within a year of making his first-team debut, Joe was on his way to Leeds United, and a fantastic career that saw him become the only Scot to score in three World Cup Finals tournaments, a feat that is unlikely ever to be emulated. Davie soon began to establish himself as a first-team regular. He came to Cappielow when they had players like Bobby Collins, Gerry Sweeney and Joe Mason. He remembers Sweeney and Mason in particular as players who loved a carry on but when the chips were down were excellent professionals who protected the young players on the field.

Morton First Division champions 1977–78. Back row, left to right: Neil Orr, George Anderson, Barry Evans, Denis Connaghan, Andy Ritchie, John Goldthorpe, Tommy Veitch. Front row: Jim Holmes, Charlie Brown, Davie Hayes, Bobby Russell, Jimmy Miller, Billy Thomas.

Determination is writ large on Davie Hayes's face as he chases Ian Scanlon of Aberdeen.

The right-back position had been a bit of a problem for Morton since Johnny Boyd left the club in 1967, with several players such as John Loughlin, Danny Ferguson, Gerry Sweeney and John Murray occupying the berth. By the beginning of the 1971–72 season, however, Davie had seen off all pretenders and would be a constant fixture for the next 12 seasons. His first goal arrived at the end of the 1972–73 season; a long distance shot against Kilmarnock. It would be almost five years until his next goals for the club, but they were amongst the most important goals ever scored at Cappielow.

Davie's arrival as a first-team regular unfortunately coincided with a downturn in the club's fortunes. Morton could not continue to sell their best players and compete in the top half of the League. From about 1971–72 most seasons were spent in the bottom six of the League, with usually a late rally toward the end of the season hoisting the club clear from the relegation area.

After we lost the likes of Bobby Collins, Gerry Sweeney and Joe Mason, we struggled for a few seasons. Up to about 1975 it was a bit of a struggle. Then Joe Gilroy came in briefly as manager and we picked up a bit. And then Benny came.

Benny Rooney was appointed player-manager of Morton at the start of the 1976–77 season and began what Davie describes as 'the best years of my career'. He almost immediately installed Davie as his captain. 'I think I was similar to Benny as a player. Benny was a hard player. He would never give up; he was a fighter. I had obviously played against him a fair few times. Maybe he saw something similar in me.'

Benny's decision to make Davie Hayes his captain turned out to be an inspired choice as Davie revelled in his new role. In his second season in charge Rooney had assembled a side that soon established a lead at the top of the First Division. Driven on by Hayes, Morton found themselves at the top of the League, one point ahead of Hearts and three ahead of Dundee with two matches left. A home midweek fixture with Airdrie was the second last match. Victory would guarantee promotion, and almost certainly the championship.

The match was possibly Davie Hayes's finest in a Morton jersey. A nervous Morton side had conceded an early goal, when in the 33rd minute Davie picked up the ball in his own half and surged forward in typical style. This time, however, there was no danger of a trademark wayward cross as Davie passed inside to Tommy Veitch, who crossed the ball for Jimmy Miller to nod down to Davie who had continued his run. Davie finished the move with a low shot into the net, and the Cappielow crowd went wild! The goal settled Morton's nerves, but with 10 minutes to go the sides were still level until John Goldthorpe made it 2–1. A penalty from Andy Ritchie sealed victory and promotion. One newspaper headline said it all the next day: 'Davie Hayes Leads Morton to the Premier League'.

It had been a team effort with some glorious individual performances from Ritchie and Mark McGhee, but the contribution of hardened pros like Davie, George Anderson and Tommy Veitch should not be underestimated. After the match Benny Rooney paid tribute to Davie's role in the Airdrie game. 'Nobody has more spirit than Davie. It was fitting that he was the player who set us on the road.'

Today, Davie jokes about his goal against Airdrie, claiming that the ball hit his knee, rolled down his shin, and ended up in the net off his big toe, but the truth was Morton could not have done it without him. He led by example throughout the season as if it was his own personal mission to deliver Premier League football. Davie may not have been a prolific goalscorer, but he did start many moves with his unflagging overlapping down the right flank. Unfortunately, the end product did not always match the build up, as many of his crosses tended to end up in the crowd behind the goal. It led to much good-natured ribbing for Davie, but his crossing did

Morton in 1982. Back row, left to right: Andy Ritchie, Joe McLaughlin, John Reynolds, Graham Kyle, Roy Baines, Roddy Hutchinson, John Marr, Martin Doak. Middle row: Eddie Morrison (reserve team coach), Eddie McNab, Alistair Maitland, Gary Dickie, Ian Cochrane, Jim Duffy, Bernie Slaven, Bobby Houston, Joe Gillies, John O'Neil, Mike Jackson (assistant manager). Front row: Willie Gray (trainer), Danny Docherty, Eddie Gavigan, Jim Holmes, Benny Rooney (manager), David Hayes, John McNeil, Jim Rooney, Barney Jensen (reserve coach).

improve later in his career, and as George Anderson says, 'The reason a lot of Davie's crosses would overshoot was because he knew that a low hard ball across the face of the goal was hard to defend against and that was the type of cross he was trying to achieve and sometimes he just gave them too much.'

And so the honour of being Morton's first captain in the Premier League fell to Davie as he led his side out against Celtic at Cappielow in August 1978. Everything had fallen into place for Davie.

There's no doubt that the team we had at Cappielow for the first couple of years in the Premier League was the best team in all my time there. We had a good balance and some excellent players. From a personal point of view, I think I was at my peak between 25 and 28, and it was the most enjoyable period of my career. There was a lot of talk about going full-time: whether that would have helped us, I don't know. We would certainly have been more organised and allowed us more time to work on our weakness, our routines, free kicks, etc. But what we achieved with a part-time squad was pretty remarkable. When we went top of the Premier we just didn't have the pool of players to sustain it. We were just that wee bit short. In the semi against Aberdeen we were terrible in the first half but gave them a doing in the second, and Neil Orr had a goal disallowed and I still don't know why. The semi against Rangers…well, what actually happened was Rangers tried to mix it with us, and we got involved in a kicking match. If we had just concentrated on the football we would have played them off the park.

For countless matches in Morton colours the highlight for many supporters was the duel between Davie and the many talented wingers of the time.

When I was in the Premier League most teams would play with one winger, and it always seemed to be a left-winger. That's why Homer [Jim Holmes] used to enjoy himself so much. He would have the whole of his side of the park to himself. So, just about every week I was directly up against somebody like Davie Cooper, Eamonn Bannon or Ian Scanlon. Sometimes they would have good days, other days I would just be better. Playing against the skilful types like Cooper didn't bother me too much, it was the pacy guys like Willie Johnston that gave me most bother. After a while I learned the best way to play against them was to close them down. So I would close mark them and try to stop them from turning. I enjoyed playing against Cooper because Benny would tell everybody just to leave him to me because if you surrounded Cooper with loads of players, he would just drop his shoulder and jink away from them. But I would just stand off him, watch the ball and jockey him, and it worked – well some of the time.

DAVIE HAYES

Mention of Ian Scanlon brings back memories of an incident in the League Cup semi-final at Hampden in 1979 against Aberdeen. Davie had embarked on one of his overlapping runs on Hampden's wide open surface, running outside Scanlon along the touchline when Scanlon, with the ball nowhere near, body checked him, taking Davie right out of the game. It was very much the biter bit and a sheepish Scanlon apologised to Davie after the match. 'Ian Scanlon is actually a very nice guy and he apologised to me later. If it had been the other way around I would not have thought twice about doing what he did. Fergie would probably have killed him if he hadn't.'

Davie himself was known as a rather robust type of player, but in five seasons in the Premier League he only missed one match through suspension. Slightly tongue-in-cheek, Davie remembers the attitude towards defenders during his peak years.

In those days you were allowed two or three kicks at an opponent before they would book you. The tackle from behind was a grey area when I was playing. You weren't really allowed to tackle from behind, but certain referees would let it go if you got the ball. I picked up bookings for tackles of course, but in my earlier days most of my problems with referees were for mouthing. I think I was sent off three or four times in my career, but a couple of them were for swearing. I was always an aggressive player – that was my strength, and I hated being beaten. I didn't model myself on anyone. I liked Terry Cooper of Leeds and I grew up watching Rangers so I suppose I was a Bobby Shearer type. John Greig was a player I admired, although after I played against him a few times I discovered he wasn't as tough as I thought.

Davie remembers some of the characters at Cappielow with great affection.

I remember a game when Billy McLaren and Roddie Hutchison went for the same ball and ran into each other and Benny was going daft in the dug out, so Hutch gives Billy a mouthful and big Billy doesn't say anything. Ten minutes later big Hutch beats two men and scores from 20 yards, an Andy Ritchie goal. We all went over to congratulate him and Billy says, 'Well done big man', and Hutch goes to shake his hand and big Billy punches him on the jaw!

Benny Rooney, for me personally, definitely helped my career. When he first came he went through a purple patch, like a lot of managers do. He just seemed to pick the right type of player. He had the basis of a good side and he added four or five players and that got us promotion, then he knew he had to get another couple for the Premier. We trained so hard and were really fit. No team ever ran over the top of us. I thought Benny was very hard done by when the club got rid of him. The directors were just looking for a way out because they had sold all the players.

Davie's last two seasons at Cappielow were blighted by injury and he only managed to play in 16 games. His last season, 1983–84, had a happy ending for the club as they won the First Division title and promotion back to the Premier League. For Davie though it was bittersweet, as he only managed four games in the League campaign. He found it hard to maintain full fitness, with

The Morton squad in 1972. Davie Hayes is seated, extreme left. Back row, left to right: J. Murphy, G Christensen, B. Osborne, G. Anderson, J. Fallon, S. Rankin, D. Laughton, D. Gillies, C. Shevlane. Front row: D. Hayes, C. Watson, J. Lumsden, S. Chalmers, J. Mason, N. McNab, J. Clark, E. Smith (manager).

ankle and knee injuries, and began to suffer from arthritis. He also did not see eye to eye with Tommy McLean, who freed Davie on the last day of the season just as Morton won promotion back to the Premier League. Davie and McLean had played against each other on countless occasions during their long careers – not always amicably. 'Wee Tommy and me didn't get on. It's possible I kicked him once too often when he was playing with Rangers!'

Ironically, McLean himself would be gone from Cappielow before long. He did however pay a nice tribute to Davie in the press saying, 'I regret having to let him go. He has been a first-class servant to Morton and has always given me 100 percent.' McLean was not saying anything that had not been obvious throughout Davie's career.

Davie had played over 450 matches for the club and his 354 League appearances stood as a post-war record until surpassed by Jim Holmes a couple of years later. In all those matches he only scored three goals, but the goal he scored against Airdrie on that memorable night in April 1978 was without doubt one of the most significant goals in Morton's history. Davie scored one other goal that season, again an all-important one – the winning goal in a 2–1 victory over Montrose on Hogmanay. There was also a nice memory for him when he scored in Allan McGraw's testimonial against Middlesbrough. Put through one on one with the goalkeeper he took the ball round him with all the aplomb of Zico at his peak before slotting it home. Unfortunately, all that effort and skill took its toll on 'Hannibal' and he had to limp off shortly afterwards, but it remains a nice memory for Davie all the same.

So why the soubriquet 'Hannibal'? Footballers are not exactly imaginative in their choice of nicknames – think 'Durranty' and 'Coisty' – but 'Hannibal' at least showed that the Morton players were aware of what was popular on television in the early 1970s. *Alias Smith and Jones* was a very successful Western series on BBC2, and one of the characters was called Hannibal Heyes. Although it was a different spelling, it seemed to fit Davie to a tee.

After leaving Morton, Davie had a short spell at Queen of the South and then Benny Rooney signed him for Partick Thistle. But by then the injuries had taken their toll. 'I think, really, my legs just went. I obviously played quite a physical game and by then they weren't quite up to playing at that level.'

Davie then stepped down to the junior grades, playing for several clubs. Johnstone Burgh and Blantyre Vics were just two clubs who benefited from his experience. Davie then played at amateur level for many years and remarkably played on until he was 47, only giving the game up when he suffered a cruciate injury.

Given Davie's love of the club and the service that he gave, it seems inconceivable that he was not given a testimonial. Both Davie and George Anderson were given an award from the supporters' club, and were given the standard promise from the directors of the time that they would be well looked after. Sadly, nothing was forthcoming, reflecting the climate of the time pre-Bosman that footballers were mere commodities. It also reflected badly on the custodians of the club at that time. Davie admits though that Morton did pay quite well for a part-time club, at least when they were in the Premier League. They also had a particularly rewarding bonus scheme. Nevertheless, the manner of his departure did hurt him at the time.

Davie still retains his affection for the club, however, and is always delighted when he meets fans who remember him from one of the most exciting periods in the club's history. He still keeps in touch with many of his old teammates and is very keen to help arrange some form of get together of Benny Rooney's side. His former teammates are in no doubt about Davie's worth to the club over the years. Neil Orr said, 'Davie was the archetypal solid full-back. He worked so hard up and down that right side; he was always willing to support the attack. He was a great tackler, gave 100 percent and always led by example.'

Mark McGhee, of course, enjoyed playing with Davie, but also experienced the dubious pleasure of opposing him many times with Aberdeen.

Well, you don't get full-backs like Davie any more. Full-backs now are much more skilful! Davie was totally uncompromising. He didn't really care what was going on in the rest of the field, just as long as his immediate opponent didn't get the better of him. When I played against him, there is no doubt he did intimidate you. It wasn't just me he kicked, if the man got between him and the ball then he was fair game. He was outstanding the season we won the League.

Mike Jackson said:

I don't think we'll ever see the likes of Davie Hayes and George Anderson again. They were the last of a dying breed. They were Morton through and through. They loved the club and loved playing for it. They were great pros and did everything they were asked. Great Morton players, who typified the hard-working Morton image.

Although Jim Holmes has the enduring image of the quintessential attacking full-back, Jim himself thinks Davie is due some credit in that regard.

Hannibal set up a lot of moves with his overlapping; he liked to take guys on. His best quality though was his determination. He never, ever gave up. I remember a match against Rangers at Ibrox. Davie Cooper turned him inside and out three times in the one movement, but Davie kept at him, and when Cooper took him on again Davie got the tackle in and blocked the cross. That was typical of his tenaciousness.

Jim Duffy remembers how Davie actually relished receiving a short pass, whereas others would have moaned about being played into trouble. 'Davie used to actually ask me to play it short. His favourite phrase was, "Play it short, he's stupid enough to go for it." This was so he could crunch his opponent, who I have to say was usually Frank McGarvey!'

Joe Jordan says that it was always felt that Davie would move on, so with so many Morton players sold off during Davie's time at the club, was there ever any possibility of a move for him?

There was talk of some interest from down south, but I don't think I was suited to playing in England. I was a bit too small. If I'd been a couple of inches taller, but by and large most defenders in England are six footers. Anyway, I was quite happy where I was. You knew that if you were any good there was a chance Hal would sell you on. I remember big Stan Rankin answered the phone one day saying, 'Hello welcome to the Cappielow sales room', and Hal had picked up the other extension and heard this, and he came thundering in demanding to know who it was that had said it. Hal was great, even if he didn't know too much about the football side of things. He would come out with some great stuff like the day he told us to play 'cowboy soccer'. He said, 'Right boys, today I want you to score a couple of early goals and win the match. It's called cowboy soccer. Bang! Bang! And the game's dead!'

It could be that Davie was so indelibly linked with Morton that other clubs just took it for granted that he would always be there. That is the way it seemed and for Davie Hayes that is the way it was. He says simply, 'I absolutely loved playing football and I loved playing for Morton. At the end of the day I've got my memories, great memories and nobody can ever take that away from me.'

Morton players enjoying their time away on tour, with a smiling Davie Hayes at the front.

Morton playing statistics: (League, League Cup, Scottish Cup)

Season	Appearances	Goals
1969–70	3 +1sub	0
1970–71	9	0
1971–72	33	0
1972–73	37	1
1973–74	44	0
1974–75	39	0
1975–76	32	0
1976–77	44	0
1977–78	36	2
1978–79	37	0
1979–80	30	0
1980–81	37	0
1981–82	42	0
1982–83	9 +1sub	0
1983–84	5 +2sub	0

Chapter 7

George Anderson
Solid as a Rock

Can there be a better feeling than playing for the club that you have supported since you were a small boy? George Anderson experienced that feeling at the tender age of 16, stepping from the classroom to the football field with consummate ease. Born and raised in Greenock's next-door neighbour, Port Glasgow, George was still a pupil of Port Glasgow High when he made his Morton debut. Before he was 17 he had played in Morton sides that had triumphed at Ibrox and Molineux. At 18, he was on the bench for Scotland against the reigning world champions Brazil at the Maracana Stadium. At one stage the football world was George's for the taking. If, ultimately his career did not ever again reach the exalted heights he achieved as a teenager, he became one of Morton's most important and fondly remembered players of the 1970s, the rock of the Morton defence.

George Anderson was born on Christmas Day 1953, and with four brothers, all of whom played football from an early age, George always had a ball at his feet. His brothers favoured other teams, but for George it was always Morton. Aged nine, he was captivated by 'Hal's Heroes' and attended the 1963 Scottish League Cup Final against Rangers. The following year the arrival of Erik Sorensen sparked off the 'Scandinavian Invasion' and helped make Cappielow a special place for George.

Going to Cappielow was something different, rather than the old Rangers-Celtic thing. I believed that you should support your local team and it just moved on from that. The side that won promotion in 1964 and reached the League Cup Final was the first Morton side that I really remember, and of course everyone of that era can recite the side off by heart. It was a great side, but probably the player who made the biggest impression on me was John Madsen, who arrived the following season. He was a centre-half, very solid, and quickly became my favourite player. I also liked Preben Arentoft and I can remember watching the likes of Per Bartram and Borge Thorup when they first came over. They then moved down to Crystal Palace and I ended up playing with them when they came back up.

George played for his primary school team and, as he got older, Port Glasgow High School and local youth side Port Glasgow Rovers. Primarily a defender, he was also a useful centre-forward and midfield player, but centre-half or sweeper was his preferred position.

In February 1970, he played in a trial match at Cappielow. The next day, coach Eric Smith turned up at George's door and informed his father that he wanted to sign George. George did not need asking twice and signed. One week later George played his first reserve match and a few days later was on the bench for the first team at Parkhead against Celtic. George came on after an hour in a 4–0 defeat against a Celtic team with 10 members of the side that would play three months later in the European Cup Final. By the end of the season George had managed two starts and three substitute appearances. He played in the winning side against Rangers at Ibrox in the last game of the season, while still at school. The season did not end with the defeat of Rangers. The European Youth Tournament was held in Scotland that summer and George was named in the pool alongside some notable contemporaries such as Alfie Conn, Derek Parlane and Jim Leishman. George played midfield in the third-place play-off match and scored one of the goals in a 2–0 victory. It was a dramatic and meteoric introduction to professional football.

It was fantastic. I remember having to tell my PE teacher that I couldn't play for the school team as I had signed for Morton. I was actually getting paid to do something that I loved, that my mates would have paid to do. But behind it all were my brothers, who helped keep my feet on the ground. My dad went to every match, home and away, and he was a real steadying influence.

The following season George established himself as a first-team regular, playing 23 out of 34 League matches and scoring his first Morton goal against St Johnstone in December 1970. He had made a huge impression with his no-nonsense tackling, ability in the air and highly developed positional sense. He was also playing alongside some decent defenders in Stan Rankin and Billy Gray. 'Hal would play the numbers game. A lot of times I would wear the number 11 jersey, playing twin centre-half with big Stan Rankin. Stan and I would pick up the strikers, and Billy Gray would play sweeper.'

One of George's first matches for Morton was against Kilmarnock at Rugby Park in October 1970 on the same day that another 16 year old, Derek Johnstone, scored the winning goal against Celtic in the League Cup Final. George deputised in goal for the last 30 minutes when Leif Nielsen sustained the injury that effectively finished his career. George's first action was to immediately pick the ball out of the net, as 'Ton trailed 2-1, but his calm performance between the posts inspired the side to a 2–2 draw.

All I remember was that it was pouring and it was freezing, and the last place I wanted to be was standing in goal. Normally, Gerry Sweeney would have taken over, but Eric Smith decided to keep him outfield and stuck me in. I don't remember much about it, but I took over in goal a couple of times after that as well.

Days after the Kilmarnock match George flew to Iceland to represent Scotland Under-18s. The big games came thick and fast when, one week later, George and the equally youthful Davie Hayes played against Wolves at Molineux in the Texaco Cup. George had arrived and by the end of that season his form was so good that Hal Stewart was able to sell Billy Gray, who was acknowledged as Morton's most accomplished defender to Dundee United. Gray had given sterling service for six seasons, but the move backfired somewhat when Stan Rankin was injured early in season 1971–72. However, Hal Stewart had already pulled off something of a coup when in the summer of 1971 he secured the signature of Lisbon Lions' Steve Chalmers and John Clark. George pays due credit to Clark for helping his progress.

When I first signed for Morton, Bobby Collins was there playing and coaching, and I had a season or so playing alongside John Clark and Stevie Chalmers. So, I was very lucky to play with these guys. You couldn't fail to learn from them. Playing at centre-half with John Clark as sweeper, I learned a lot. John wasn't loud or demonstrative, but he didn't need to be to pass on his knowledge.

George was again a fixture for Scottish Youth in 1971 in a side that included ex-Notts Forest and Scotland winger John Robertson. He was still young enough to play

Morton in 1979. George Anderson is third from right, back row. The rest of the team are, back row, left to right: Jim Holmes, Jim Rooney, Jimmy Miller, Roy Baines, Andy Ritchie, Cammy Melville, Roddie Hutchinson, Ally Scott. Front row: John McNeill, Neil Orr, Joe McLaughlan, Bobby Thomson, Jon Wilkie, Billy MacLaren, Jim Tolmie.

for a third year running in 1972 when he captained the side, which contained Kenny Burns and Frank Gray, through the European Youth Finals qualifiers.

Just before the Finals we played England in Birmingham and won 1–0, so I can always say I've captained a Scotland side that's beaten the English. We then flew to Spain for the Finals, winning two of our group games but just failed to qualify from our group on goal difference.

George's form began to attract interest from other clubs and Hal Stewart turned down a £50,000 bid from Aberdeen when George was still only 17. It did seem certain at that stage that George would eventually move on to a bigger club for a large fee. George's value multiplied again when in the summer of 1972, the Scotland national side, managed by Tommy Docherty, embarked on a trip to South America to play in a 'mini World Cup' tournament. There had been a couple of withdrawals due to injury and George was drafted into the squad. It was a huge honour for Morton and George personally because, despite the withdrawals, it was still a strong Scotland pool, with several members of the World Cup side of two years later travelling.

I think it was part injuries and part Tommy Docherty having a look at a couple of players for the future. Kenny Burns was supposed to go as well, but didn't make it. It was unbelievable at 18 to be involved in something like that. Training with guys like Denis Law, who was my hero, and great players like Billy Bremner, Martin Buchan and Willie Morgan were there. We trained for 10 days in Largs and then flew out to Brazil for a couple of weeks. I didn't actually play in any of the games, I was substitute, but who cares? At 18 it was an out-of-this-world experience. I was on the bench against Brazil in the Maracana Stadium. Brazil won 1–0 with a crowd of 100,000 there, and we had to leave our hotel to get there about two, two and a half hours before kick-off such was the throng of Brazilian fans on the way.

At this stage George was the most highly rated young centre-half in Scotland and it did seem only a matter of time before he moved on to a bigger club and gained further international recognition. In 1973, Jim Holton, who had just moved to Manchester United, was preferred to George in an Under-23 match. The *Daily Express* 'Voice of Football' columnist John McKenzie was moved to ask if home-grown talent was being ignored at the expense of big money English-based players, and added that George should surely be a fixture in the Scotland Under-23 side.

George was belatedly picked against Wales and teamed up with Holton. 'Big Jim played centre-half and I played sweeper, so basically all I did was pick people up – off the ground that is after Jim clattered them!'

George was also picked to play against England Under-23s, but after struggling through a game for Morton, he was forced to withdraw with flu. Then unaccountably George's career stalled. The long expected transfer to a bigger club never materialised due to a combination of injuries, bad timing and circumstances beyond George's control. In 1975, he broke a shoulder against East Fife, causing him to miss most of the 1975–76 season. On the day of his injury it is said, Hal Stewart was at Ibrox talking over a bid for George from Rangers. There was also interest from Celtic, but Jock Stein's car crash effectively put an end to that. The cruellest blow of all was probably in 1977 when a move to Birmingham City fell through when their Scottish manager Willie Bell was sacked.

Sir Alf Ramsey took over as caretaker manager and I don't think there was anyway he was going to sign a Scotsman! So I just trained with Birmingham for a couple of days and then came up the road. It probably wasn't the blow it might have been because I had another career with Scott Lithgow.

It is also probable that Hal Stewart, just like he would do in later years with Andy Ritchie, priced George out of the market, an assessment George's good friend Davie Hayes agrees with. Davie is of the opinion that Hal Stewart was looking for a fortune for George. However, it should not be suggested that George was desperate to leave Morton, but as he says himself:

As a footballer, your aim must be to play at as high a standard as possible. In hindsight it may have benefited me if I had moved on at 22 or 23; the freshness, the new challenge, etc. The danger is you get so far and then stay at that level because subconsciously you're comfortable. Perhaps you need something else to stretch you, to take you to that next level. Who knows? Jim Holmes never got a move and he was the best full-back in Scotland for so many years. If Homer had been playing for Celtic or Rangers he would have walked into the Scotland side.

That next level for George came in the summer of 1976 with the appointment of Benny Rooney as Morton manager. Benny's no-nonsense approach turned an ailing club around and, for George personally, the appointment of Benny Rooney coincided with a return to the kind of form that had made him such a highly rated player. Still only 22 when Rooney arrived, George blossomed once more and formed arguably the finest centre-back partnership ever seen at the club. Neil Orr, son of the famous Tommy, had managed a handful of games under Joe Gilroy and his promise was there for all to see. Benny Rooney gave him an extended run in his first season as manager, but Neil was still a little raw and needed a steady hand beside him. George filled the role admirably, guiding Orr through matches until by season 1977–78, Orr was one of the most important players in the side.

In August 1977, Morton set out on what would ultimately be a triumphant campaign, culminating in the First Division title and promotion to the Premier

George as part of the Scottish squad for the mini-World Cup in 1972. He is second from the right on the back row.

League for the first time. A rejuvenated George Anderson was a major player in the triumph. He was free of injury, had formed an outstanding partnership with the ever-present Orr and had added a goal touch to his all-round game. George ended the season with nine goals, almost all of them from dead balls from Andy Ritchie.

People would tell me I only had to get my head on the end of big Andy's crosses, but I would reply that it wasn't that easy, the speed that the big man would fire them at! We just seemed to have a sort of telepathy. Andy knew where I was going to run to and I knew where he was going to hit the ball.

George's nine goals were almost all vital, especially given that 'Ton eventually clinched the title on goal difference. In one remarkable seven-day period he scored in three successive League matches, all headers from Andy's corners, including a late equaliser away to Arbroath. Early in the season a goal against Montrose secured a vital point, and as the season moved to a nail-biting conclusion, he notched two in one game against St Johnstone. In the match report the next day, the *Greenock Telegraph*, not often given to hyperbole, compared George to Billy McNeill saying, 'George Anderson is far too good a player to be playing at this level of football, and what's more is determined to prove it. He commanded the air like Billy McNeill in his heyday and marshalled his defence with complete authority.'

If Andy Ritchie was the brilliant shining star of the side, and Davie Hayes was the driving force, then George was the heart and soul of a side that never gave up. The title and promotion was won against Airdrie, and a memorable season for George was complete when he won two club Player of the Year awards and was nominated for the division's Players' Player of the Year award at the season's conclusion.

Unfortunately for George he was suspended for the first match of the Premier campaign, but he was back in his regular berth the following week. Gradually, Morton adjusted to the demands of the Premier League, but in September, George damaged ankle ligaments against Hearts. Billy McLaren was brought in and with the injury George only managed 18 games that season as Morton finished a comfortable seventh. The following season with three top-class centre-backs in

George, Orr and the emerging Joe McLaughlin at the club, Benny Rooney would occasionally play all three together, or move George to full-back, or play a rotational system.

We must have been doing something right because we were top of the Premier League at Christmas. Okay, lack of depth in the pool cost us, but we thought we could go on winning. We had great confidence in each other and our own abilities. Throughout my career I played to win every match. I don't think I ever went to Parkhead or Ibrox thinking we were going to lose. It just didn't enter my mind. And never with any of Benny's teams did we go out with an inferiority complex. Benny was great for me personally and we got on really well together. We had our occasional fall-outs, but we would apologise and it would be forgotten about. Benny and Mike Jackson created a brilliant atmosphere and everyone fitted in well. Even as the team evolved and newcomers came in, they fitted in straight away. We had a lot of fun on and off the park.

Ironically, when the time did come for George to leave the club he had always supported, it was when he had resolved within himself that he would spend the rest of his career with Morton.

George Anderson with Scotland in 1972.

I had been at the club for 10 or 11 years and basically I was looking for some sort of commitment from them. I was willing to sign another contract for four or five years, and that would have taken me to 32. I would have spent half my life there. All I was looking for was a testimonial that would perhaps guarantee me a certain amount of money. The chairman promised that he would look after me, but wasn't willing to put anything down on paper. So, when I heard Airdrie were looking for a centre-half, I decided that my best option was to move. I really didn't want to leave, but the commitment from the club wasn't there. Benny didn't think I was looking for anything

I wasn't entitled to, he was great about it and there was no fall-out with him. So really that was the only reason I left Morton. I was prepared to commit the rest of my career to them. I know Joe McLaughlin had established himself, but that wasn't why I left. I had seen off threats before and I was still in Benny's plans. I wasn't playing for the money. I had a good job outside football. I was playing because I loved football and Morton was my team, but I had a great time at Airdrie. I played with them in the Premier League, and won a couple of Player of the Year awards.

Ex-Ranger Bobby Watson was the manager who signed George for a fee in the region of £37,000, apparently after consultation with his friend Alex Ferguson. George played exactly 100 League games with Airdrie, only leaving in 1985 when Ally McLeod could not promise him a regular game, despite claiming in the newspapers that George was actually his best player!

When the chance came to return to Cappielow in 1985, George jumped at it. 'Allan McGraw had just taken over and was looking for an experienced player to coach the reserves and help out in the first team when necessary, and it was a great opportunity for me.'

Once again George provided a steadying influence as McGraw set about restructuring the club after a disastrous season in the Premier League. George actually played in 16 matches in his first season back and once again was able to pass on the benefit of his experience to other young players, including a young Jim Hunter, fresh out of juvenile football. His last game for Morton's first team was the first match of the 1986–87 season, which was also notable as Rowan Alexander's first.

George sustained a knee injury in the first half and Rowan took over: the start of one great Morton career and the end of another. Thereafter, George concentrated on coaching the reserves and, as a Morton supporter first and foremost, he celebrated when McGraw's side won the First Division in that season and suffered when they were relegated again the next season. Restructuring of the backroom staff resulted in George leaving Cappielow in 1988. A spell in charge of Port Glasgow Juniors followed, but George found after a lifetime in the senior game that some junior players did not share his ideas and expectations, and he left the club after a season in charge. Since then George has not returned to the game that was his life for 20 years. One thing that has endured, however, is his love of Morton Football Club. Still very much a supporter, he has experienced the highs and lows of the last few seasons, and is still a regular on the terraces.

George looks back on his career and the type of player that he was with great candour.

Probably my major stumbling block was that I wasn't the tallest. I would have liked to have been three or four inches taller. So I had to make up for that with timing and physical presence. I never went out to hurt anyone, but Eric Smith always told me that when you tackled someone, they stayed tackled! As far as I'm concerned, for a centre-half a yellow card is par for the course because you have to go where others don't go. I was ordered off three times early in my career, but as I grew more experienced I learned how far I could go. Of course referees in those days were stronger. With Tiny Wharton and Bobby Davidson you knew where you stood. You had the utmost respect for them. And with Ian Foote, I knew I was going to be booked, because every time he refereed Morton he booked me. Wee Davie [Hayes] was no shrinking violet either, and part of our job was to win the ball and give it to guys who could do different things with it.

George has no real regrets about his career and feels proud to have been an important part of Morton for so long, and to have played in some distinguished company.

I played in a golden era for Scottish football. When I started out Celtic still had most of the Lisbon Lions and every side had good strikers. Never mind Celtic and Rangers. Hibs had Alan Gordon and Jim O'Rourke, wee Joe [Harper] was at Aberdeen, Hearts had Donald Ford and later in my career even the lesser teams if you

*like had real tough strikers. St Mirren had Doug Somner and Airdrie had Sandy
Clark. I had some good tussles with Andy Gray, but I would say Dalglish was the best
player I played against. I respected these guys, but I was never in awe of them.*

*I don't know if I could play today with all the diving that goes on though, because
I can't stand cheats. I also don't know how I would get on with the lack of physical
contact now. The powers that be are trying to protect the ball players, but I don't see
many 'Jinky' Johnstones coming through. When I played it was knock for knock and
then shake hands afterwards. Playing against tough customers like Alex MacDonald
and Drew Busby, I would kick them and they would kick me, but there were no
vendettas. We would shake hands after the game and that's the way it should be. The
only bother I had was with Malcolm MacDonald who refused to shake my hand after
a match against Newcastle. I was a physical player, but over the years I was probably
injured just as much by opponents doing things to me that others didn't see.*

It is impossible for anyone to have played for Morton in Hal Stewart's time and
not have a story to tell of the legendary Hal.

*Hal's favourite ploy was going to Ibrox or Parkhead and we would always arrive
without something like a pair of boots. We would then borrow a pair from them and
Hal would say, 'Just send us the bill', knowing that Celtic and Rangers would never*

Morton Football Club in 1980.

send out a bill for a pair of boots. So every time we went to Ibrox or Parkhead, somebody would get a new pair of boots! But they didn't mind because they knew that if ever they were looking for some match practice, Hal would fix up a closed door friendly with them.

Having made his first-team debut at 16, and having played 200 matches by the time he was 21, the lack of young players coming through in Scottish football is of great concern to George.

When I first broke into the first team at Morton, just about every club brought through good young players at an early age. Now it doesn't happen. Young players don't get a chance because of the amount of foreigners in the game. And now we barely have an Old Firm player in the Scotland side. There should be a limit of, say, five foreign players imposed and perhaps we would see the benefits to our own players. At Morton we always seemed to have one or two local players in the side. Through the years there was Joe Harper, Neil McNab, Neil Orr, John McNeil, Charlie Brown, Joe McLaughlin, but we seem to have lost that now as well.

Jim Holmes played side by side with George and this is his assessment of him.

George had a great physical presence. He was very strong in the tackle, had great timing in the air both defending and attacking, and centre-forwards certainly knew he was there. He made good decisions. He always seemed to know when to take a touch and when to put the ball in the stand. He formed a great partnership with Neil Orr.

By a conservative estimate George had over a dozen different centre-back partners in his 11 years at Cappielow, but he does not hesitate in naming Neil Orr as his favourite. 'We complemented each other very well. We developed a kind of telepathy. In the early days Neil would man mark, and I would cover for him, but as he matured and with his exceptional pace he became the ideal sweeper.'

Long-time admirer Arthur Montford believes George's loyalty to the club may

George Anderson in action

have held him back. 'I always thought that George could and should have played on a much higher stage. Possibly his affection for the club prevented him from moving on to bigger things.'

Mark McGhee considers George the cornerstone of a great Morton back four. 'George was as uncompromising as Davie Hayes, but he was a footballer as well. I would put him in the Willie Miller bracket. Like Willie he wasn't the biggest or the quickest, but his greatest quality was his consistency.'

The last word on George should perhaps go to Benny Rooney.

I knew when I came to Morton that George had been a great servant. Any doubts I might have had regarding his height were quickly dispelled. He became a great stalwart. He was a tower of strength in the season we were promoted especially. When George played well he helped the defence settle down. He was magnificent during the long unbeaten run that we had. Balls that you thought he would never win, he just won them, and he kept us in a lot of matches. He was a tremendous player for me.

Morton fans would ideally see the best of George Anderson on a typically cold, wet Greenock day in the middle of winter with barely a blade of grass on Cappielow's mud bath of a park. George would be up against a big name striker of the day, perhaps Malcolm McDonald of Newcastle or Colin Stein of Rangers. Reputations meant nothing to George and the bigger the name the harder the tackles. George Anderson was the perfect exponent of the slide tackle, and when George tackled someone, they stayed tackled!

Morton playing statistics: (League, League Cup, Scottish Cup)

Season	Appearances	Goals
1969–70	2 +3subs	0
1970–71	24 +1sub	1
1971–72	41	1
1972–73	37	2
1973–74	35 +1sub	1
1974–75	29 +2subs	0
1975–76	14	1
1976–77	42	2
1977–78	45	9
1978–79	18	3
1979–80	25 +4subs	2
1980–81	6	1
1985–86	18 +2subs	2
1986–87	1	0

Neil Orr

It is impossible to talk about the Morton defence during the Benny Rooney years without mention of Neil Orr – surely one of the classiest defenders ever seen at Cappielow. Neil was born in 1959 in Gourock and as the son of Tommy Orr, one of Morton's greatest ever players, it was perhaps inevitable that one day he would wear the blue and white hoops.

Neil's talent was evident from a young age and he came through the juvenile ranks, signing an 'S' form for Morton at 14. Sadly, his father had passed away shortly before. Neil signed professional forms with Morton when he turned 16 and before long was challenging for a first-team spot. By 17 he was a regular, forming a great partnership with George Anderson. Neil was a key player in Morton's ascendancy from struggling First Division side to Premier League leaders, all achieved within the space of three years. At 19 he won the first of seven Under-21 caps and he won a League cap under Jock

Neil Orr in action.

Stein in 1980. His great assets were his pace and powers of recovery in the tackle.

By the 1981–82 season, although Morton's overall form had slipped, Neil had formed another excellent partnership with Joe McLaughlin, and continued to grow in stature. He was also gaining admiring glances from bigger clubs. After one particular match against Dundee United, an astute a judge as Jim McLean, who had international centre-backs in Paul Hegarty and David Narey, was moved to ask, 'If I was Morton manager I would want to know why Neil Orr is not in the Scotland side. He's a class act.'

Ask Benny Rooney now of his memories of Neil Orr and he positively glows. 'It's hard to say who your best player was but Neilly was something special. I thought he was a cert for the Scotland side, but he was bugged by a hamstring injury and that held him back a bit.'

Neil did seem a certainty to be named in Scotland's World Cup squad of 40 for Spain, but was overlooked. After all, he played for Morton didn't he? Looking back, however, a transfer was inevitable. When it did come, in 1982, it was out of the blue.

I was only informed about West Ham's interest on the Saturday morning and by midnight I was a West Ham player. I met John Lyall and Eddie Bailey in Glasgow airport, and the deal was done. No agents in those days of course. I dealt with it all myself. Looking back, at times like that I would have liked to pick up the phone and speak to my dad. I wasn't actually aware of the financial problems the club had, although we hadn't had a home game for a few weeks because of the weather. I hadn't been looking for a move; I was very happy. I had three years of a four-year contract left.

With my background I was always a Morton fan. I can remember watching guys like Stan Rankin and George Anderson from the terracing and then actually playing with them. So it was a dream come true to play for Morton. But it was a chance to move from part-time to full-time with quite a high-profile club. They had won the FA Cup two seasons previously and had just lost to Liverpool in the League Cup Final. I had played with Ray Stewart in the Under-21s and he had obviously told me all about them. I made my debut against Manchester United and was directly up against Frank Stapleton. Just about every First Division club at that time had class strikers. I played against Dalglish and Rush, and Keegan and Channon at Southampton, and played against Frank Worthington who was getting on a bit, but was still a class act.

Neil spent a successful five and a half year spell with the Hammers, although the full caps that seemed his by right never materialised. In his early days in London the centre-back partnership of Billy Bonds and Alvin Martin was firmly established, so Neil rarely got a chance in his favoured back-four position, and was used predominantly in midfield. He was also troubled by recurrent hamstring injuries. Neil returned to Scotland in 1987 for a six-year spell at Hibs, winning a League Cup winners' medal. He wound down an almost 20-year career, during which he played around 600 games, with St Mirren and Queen of the South.

Mike Jackson described Neil Orr as follows.

Neil Orr was an absolute diamond. He always wanted to be the first at everything he did. He never cut corners at training or during matches. He did everything that was asked of him and did it well. A wonderful player to work with.

Davie Hayes said:

What made Neilly a really good player was his recovery rate, which was second to none. His pace was phenomenal; those big long legs would eat up the ground. He was sharp and had a good football brain. He was unlucky with injuries when he went to West Ham.

Neil himself acknowledges that he played for Morton at the best possible time.

I am grateful to many people for the help they gave me at Morton. Joe Gilroy gave me my first chance and Benny was very supportive and patient, and Mike Jackson was a big influence as well. Experienced players like George Anderson, Jim Holmes, Tommy Veitch, Eddie Morrison and Jim Townsend were a big help in the early days, and it was great just to be on the same field as Andy Ritchie. He could do everything, even in training. His range of passing was fantastic. To this day I have still never seen anyone as skilful. All in all it was a great time to be at Morton, but we should have gone full-time. The club didn't realise how much Benny could achieve.

Morton playing statistics: (League, League Cup, Scottish Cup)

Season	Appearances	Goals
1975–76	4	0
1976–77	23 +4subs	0
1977–78	45	0
1978–79	45	1
1979–80	45	1
1980–81	41	0
1981–82	22	0

Chapter 8

Jim Duffy
Cappielow Grit

What is it about Morton and a certain type of defender? From the club's early days through to their 1922 Cup-winning side and Jock McIntyre, to Jimmy Whyte, skipper of the 1948 Cup Final side, to the record-breaking 1963–64 side and Johnny Boyd, to the more recent 'heart on the sleeve' stalwarts Hayes and Anderson, the club seems to have bred an assembly line of resolute, almost heroic defenders. All of the aforementioned embodied the Cappielow grit that Joe Harper remembers encountering every time he came back to Greenock with Aberdeen and Hibs. Possibly, this type of defender reflects the proud shipyard past of the Greenock area, with the work ethic and pride in one's work, and a job well done. They are a dying breed. In recent years think Jim Hunter and Martin Doak and, above all, think Jim Duffy.

Jim Duffy was born in 1959 in Maryhill, one of Glasgow's renowned 'schemes' – famous for its close-knit community and abrasive but kindly personality. Football was in Jim's blood. His uncle, Neil Duffy, was an excellent professional with several clubs in the 1960s, including Dundee United and Partick Thistle, and his cousin, Neil Burke, played for Aberdeen. Neil Duffy's own son, also Neil, would also have a fine career with Falkirk and Ayr in the 1980s and 1990s. So, for Jim, like so many other young kids, it was football, football and even more football. The obligatory

Jim Duffy in 1982,
in his Morton
training kit.

street games in the area known as 'The Barracks' were his breeding grounds, followed by school and youth football.

It was football morning 'til night, regardless of the weather, and it did seem to bring kids together. It was quite a tough area with rival gangs and such like, but I don't recall much bother when they all came together to play football. But playing against kids that were sometimes that bit older certainly toughened me up. With that type of background you could either develop into an aggressive player, which I suppose I was, or you could be like Charlie Nicholas, who just happened to be my next-door neighbour. And if there is such a thing as a child prodigy then Charlie was it. Sometimes our kick-abouts would be 15-a-side, and that's when guys like Charlie develop their skills. He learned how to beat a man with a dribble because there was no room to pass, whereas I learned to tackle.

In his teenage years Jim progressed to various youth sides, such as Rangers Boys Club and Lochburn Juniors, before signing for Possil YM, a boys' club famous throughout Scotland for producing innumerable young talents including Tony Fitzpatrick and Kenny Dalglish. Jim is full of praise for the people who run these boys' clubs, giving so much of their time and effort.

Guys like Davie Keegan, Jimmy Dinnie and Brian Byrne helped me so much and I owe them a huge debt. There have been so many people through the years that have helped me in their own way. As you grow up they give you little things that years later you look back and just know that they were right. John [Jocky] Thomson at Maryhill Juniors and my PE teacher, Jim Neal, were just two who gave me great encouragement. They instilled a belief and a desire in me to succeed in the game.

Aged 17, Jim signed for his local junior side Maryhill. It was, as the cliché goes, a tough learning curve in the hurly burly of junior football.

It was tough all right. I was playing against guys who had been around, some of whom were twice my age and pretty ruthless. You think some senior players are

Jim Duffy,
pictured in
1982.

tough, but these guys were different class. I loved it at the time, but looking back I can hardly believe some of the stuff that went on.

Playing as a midfielder at that stage, Jim made a huge impact in his 18 months at Maryhill and even managed a hat-trick in the Scottish Cup against Auchinleck Talbot. His form soon caught the attention of senior clubs and Hamilton and Partick Thistle expressed an interest. But after Celtic scout John Kelman had recommended him to Celtic, Jim signed for them in 1979.

Signing for Celtic wasn't so much as a dream come true as more of a surprise, as I hadn't really aspired to those heights. I thought that perhaps I would be good enough for a senior career at lower division level, so it was a complete surprise that Celtic wanted me.

It was not that the young Duffy lacked confidence in his ability – he had plenty of that. It was perhaps that he did not realise how good he was, initially at least. He was soon made captain of the Celtic reserve side that hardly lost a match for two years but, frustratingly, the first-team call-up, aside from one Glasgow Cup match, never came.

After a couple of years at Celtic I felt that I was as good as anyone at that age and I know the coaching staff did as well. I don't blame Billy McNeil for not playing me though. I got on very well with him and respected him immensely, although I wasn't in awe of him. Billy is a legend and is now a great friend. With the passing of the years I can see that it was hard for him to take a chance on me as Celtic have to win every match. By this stage however I was 22 and wanted first-team football, so when the chance came to join Morton I grabbed it.

In February 1982, Morton sold their star defender Neil Orr to West Ham for £350,000. A replacement was required and 'Ton manager Benny Rooney targeted Jim. Benny was a good friend of Billy McNeil and Jim signed initially on a month's loan.

Jim receives a plaque presented by Cup sponsors the Scottish Health Education Group, after being nominated 'Mr Superfit' by journalists present at his side's Scottish Cup third-round tie at Cappielow in 1985. Also in the picture are director of SHEG, Stanley Mitchell (left) and Sir Simpson Stevenson, chairman of the Common Services agency.

Benny had pulled a few rabbits out of the hat, like signing Andy Ritchie for a song and bringing Roy Baines back from Celtic, and sometimes that can work against you. He was always under pressure to wheel and deal in the transfer market, and yet again when he lost Neil Orr he had to bring someone in to do a job.

Jim was a totally different style of player from Neil Orr, but in his first two matches he completely won over a Morton support reeling from the loss of yet another star player. A couple of weeks after Orr left, Jim made his Morton debut against Partick Thistle in a 0–0 draw and hardly lost a tackle all day.

After a couple of games of my loan spell, I knew that I wanted to stay. I now had the taste for first-team football, although Celtic wanted to keep me, and had offered me a new contract. I will never regret my time at Parkhead though. It gave me a platform to build on.

Whether Celtic ever regretted letting Jim go is another matter all together. Had he stayed on at Parkhead, his time would surely have come, and saved the club many expensive follies in the transfer market.

However, Jim does not believe in looking back with anger or regret on any stage of his career. For him, everything that happened during his career was just part of a huge rollercoaster.

Jim had joined a Morton side that had probably reached their pinnacle with a couple of semi-final appearances and a memorable season in 1979–80 when they had briefly topped the Premier League. The all-too-familiar transfer exodus had resulted in them losing Bobby Thomson and Jim Tolmie, as well as Orr. Although still a fixture in the Premier League, they were now found more often in the bottom half of the table than battling for European places. In Jim's first season though, they did still finish a comfortable seventh with his £25,000 transfer fee yet another masterstroke from Benny Rooney.

I think perhaps that because Morton had done so well in their first two or three seasons in the Premier, expectations had reached an unrealistic level. They were punching above their weight slightly. Benny couldn't continue to lose his best players and hope to replace them with players of equal quality.

Jim struck up an immediate partnership with centre-half Joe McLaughlin.

Joe was an ideal centre-half for me in that he attacked everything. He was great in the air, strong in the tackle and very commanding all round. My only regret was that we didn't play together longer as he was also moved on to Chelsea in my second season at the club.

Jim struck up an immediate rapport with the Cappielow crowd, who have always been quick to recognise a player who gives of his best. His no-nonsense approach and total commitment endeared him to the supporters. He settled in so quickly that it was hard to believe that prior to signing for Morton all his experience had been confined to reserve and junior football.

His tackling became the stuff of legend in the days when footballers were still allowed to tackle with vigour. To gasps of admiration and roars of approval he would launch his slight frame into challenges against players much taller and heavier than himself, like a latter day Dave MacKay, and emerge with the ball. His positional sense was highly tuned, and very near faultless, and such was Jim's form that the loss of a terrific player like Neil Orr was not as drastic as first feared.

I didn't consciously model my game on anyone, but if pushed I would say that I admired Willie Miller more than anyone in my position. He wasn't particularly strong in the air, he had only one good foot and wasn't blessed with great pace, yet he very rarely allowed himself to be exposed. He didn't just disguise his weaknesses, he totally masked them. He defended the right areas and made as few errors as possible. He absolutely dominated the penalty area and you very rarely saw him being caught on a one-on-one on the halfway line, for example. Players like Willie were worth their weight in gold.

Jim enjoyed a great rapport with the Cappielow crowd.

I think the fans could tell that I gave 100 percent and they responded to that. In all my time at Morton I never had any negative feedback from the fans. When fans see a player trying his hardest, even if he's not the greatest of players, then they respond in kind. I think I also showed that I was prepared to leave a club like Celtic, leave the comfort zone if you like, in order to further my career.

Benny Rooney and Mike Jackson, the Morton managerial duo, knew they had unearthed a diamond and now, more than 20 years later, they still look on Jim as one of their best signings. Benny Rooney describes how they had to wait to sign the player and how they quickly realised his qualities.

We were actually told about Jim when we first went into the Premier League, but we had to wait until Neil Orr moved before we could get him. And what a player he became for us – he was a revelation. Obviously I knew all about him, but he exceeded all expectations. He blended in immediately. His qualities were evident: a huge will to win, great commitment and a born leader.

Jim Duffy celebrates with Dom Sullivan at Cappielow Park.

Jim is quick to recognise the influence Benny Rooney and Mike Jackson had on his career.

I had a tremendous time at Morton. Benny and Mike were a great team and I have much to thank them for. They had a real belief in me and installed a confidence in me that sustained me throughout my career. My eternal thanks goes to these guys because without them I wouldn't have had a career. The Morton side at that time was like 11 editions of The Beano. *I always knew when I picked up big Andy's [Ritchie] or Hutchie's [Roddie Hutchison] jersey, as it would be full of cigarette burns. The atmosphere was great; they worked hard and played hard. There were some great professionals there like Jim Holmes, Jim Rooney and Davie Hayes. Benny Rooney was a bright young manager and he was lost to the game too soon. I know he had a bad time at Partick Thistle but it was a loss to the game when he left it behind.*

Unfortunately for Morton and their fans, the club could not hope to sell their best players and survive in the Premier League. In 1983, at the end of Jim's second season there, Morton were relegated. Benny Rooney and Mike Jackson were unfairly sacked and ex-Ranger Alex Miller was installed as manager. Miller only lasted a few months before moving to St Mirren and Eddie Morrison replaced him as a temporary measure. Eddie guided the side through an eight-match unbeaten run and put Morton back into the promotion race. Eddie Morrison made it clear however that he did not want the job on a permanent basis. Tommy McLean took over the reins in late November in time to guide the club to a rather improbable title win. This was a surprise given the upheaval and the comings and goings.

Jim had sometimes been used in midfield in the earlier part of the season as Morton struggled for consistency. With the departure of Miller, however, he reverted to his familiar sweeper role and was instrumental in Morton's rise to the top of the League. Jim was pressed into service of a different kind when he took over in goal from the injured Murray McDermott during a match away to Raith Rovers. Jim was not called into action much, largely due to a superb John McNeill hat-trick that knocked the stuffing out of Raith. This talented but maddeningly inconsistent player was a key man in the championship surge, scoring 17 goals. McNeill played over 300 games for Morton in 16 seasons and was listed as substitute for another 100, giving an insight into his fluctuating form.

Jim's first goal for Morton was against Kilmarnock in November 1983 at Cappielow. Morton were trailing 2–0 with five minutes left when Jim gathered the ball in his own half and galloped forward before unleashing a 30-yard drive past the Killie 'keeper. John McNeill equalised two minutes later and 'Ton had secured a vital point. Jim's one other goal that season came against Alloa in January 1984. Willie Pettigrew tried to claim a touch on Jim's cross-come-shot, but one glower from Duffy and he swiftly changed his mind!

Week by week Morton steadily clawed back long-time leaders Partick Thistle's lead and only hit the top of the League for the first time with four matches left. Promotion was achieved with a 1–0 win over Falkirk, and with three matches to go, it was neck and neck between 'Ton and Dumbarton for the championship. The title race went to the last day of the season with 'Ton a point ahead of Dumbarton. A 3–2 victory over Kilmarnock at Cappielow secured the title – something that had looked highly unlikely for a large part of the season. The League was won despite a long injury list for the majority of the season. At one stage in February, 'Ton only had 13 players to choose from and some of them, including Jim, played when injured. So it was very much a triumph against the odds. Even more improbably, given Greenock's infamous wet weather, the victory against Killie was only achieved after the fire brigade had been called in to give the bone-hard pitch a thorough soaking! 'You don't get too many medals in your career and it was a great honour for me to captain the side. The Kilmarnock game was memorable. It's one of those memories that stick with you throughout your career.'

Unfortunately, Jim's memories of the next season are bitter sweet as 'Ton struggled in the Premier League. Tommy McLean left the club to take over at Motherwell and his brother Willie was installed as manager. Although Jim personally got on well with McLean, his dour personality and the fact that he had informed the directors that he would only stay for a year did not augur well for the future. And so it proved. A lack of investment in the side ensured that the fans endured a nightmare season in which they won only four matches and conceded a century of goals.

Jim shows his trademark determination to win the ball.

It was particularly sad for the brave and resilient goalkeeper, Murray McDermott, who had been such a key figure in the previous season and had won the Player of the Year award. One man however stood out like a beacon – Jim Duffy. In every match that he played he led from the front, marshalling his beleaguered teammates against often insurmountable odds. The Morton fans had been short-changed by a board of directors unwilling or unable to generate the wherewithal and desire to sustain the club's survival in a cut-throat Premier League. Jim Duffy was not slow to voice his feelings at the time. 'I was quite critical of the board at the time. We had a mix of players, some of whom were getting on a bit, and some who were too raw and inexperienced. I was the captain and it was my job to help them.'

Jim Holmes was also part of the Morton defence in that disastrous season, and also played alongside Jim in happier times at Cappielow.

Duff was just a great defender. He made the right decisions at the right time. He knew when to attack the ball, and he knew when to sit back and push the attacker out wide. I remember countless occasions when he was outnumbered by two or even three to one, and he always seemed to get something on the ball, just enough to give the rest of the defence a chance to get back. His reading of the game was second to none, he never panicked and was always composed, and I when I played under him at Falkirk his organisation was excellent. Can you imagine how many goals we would have lost that season [1984–85] without him?

If the 1984–85 season was a disaster for Morton as a club, for Jim Duffy it was to end in personal triumph when he was voted the PFA Player of the Year. More often than not awarded to Old Firm players or to someone from a club who had had a good season, the award from his fellow professionals recognised that Jim had been outstanding for his club during a difficult season, and that he had never given up in any match.

I don't think it was a sympathy award. The fellow nominees were Frank McDougall, who had scored over 30 goals that season, Davie Cooper and Paul McStay, so it was an honour just to be mentioned in the same breath as these brilliant players. When I heard that I had won, I was gobsmacked but very proud. I treasure the award to this day and it is the only piece of memorabilia from my career that is on display in my house. Playing for Morton you always have to give that bit extra, and I always gave 100 percent, and I think my fellow pros recognised that.

But with Morton's relegation, Jim's time at Greenock had come to an end after three and a half seasons of total commitment. The impact he had made on the Morton fans was huge and when he moved on, there was no sense of animosity towards him. It was recognised that he was moving to further his career, and of course Morton were as usual selling their best asset. 'I didn't ask away as such, it was just a situation that Morton were going to have to sell their better players, and a couple of clubs were interested.'

Dundee and Hibs expressed their interest and both put in bids. Dundee's was the higher at around £65,000, and Jim plumped for Dundee, then a Premier League club. It was the beginning of a two-way love affair between Jim and the Dundee club, although it was not all plain sailing at first, as Jim readily admits. He found the step up from part-time to full-time difficult and discovered that he was not as fit as he thought he was.

Additionally, Dundee manager Archie Knox's abrasive manner jarred with him a little. He found himself trying too hard to please, with the result that he was not playing to his best form. The Dundee fans, like their Morton counterparts realised that Jim's heart was in the right place, however, and were patient with him, and he soon won them and Knox over.

For the next two seasons he was outstanding in the heart of the Dundee back four, as the side comfortably held their own in the top League. Sadly, an injury in a match at Ibrox in 1987 severely affected Jim's career. Ironically, it was not one of Jim's bone-jarring tackles that caused the injury. The simple process of catching his studs in the turf caused a fractured knee cap and a torn cartilage, as well as horrendous damage to his cruciate and remedial ligaments. Jim was told his playing career was over.

It is devastating to be told that you can no longer do the job you love doing. I was in a trance for a while, but luckily for me, my wife had just given birth to my daughter, and my son was only three, and that was my saving grace. It was a huge blow to give up playing, but my family helped me get over the disappointment.

Jim was not out of the game too long, becoming Gordon McQueen's assistant at Airdrie for a few months, before being offered the Falkirk manager's job at the age of 29 in 1989. In accepting the Falkirk job, Jim embarked on a managerial career even more tumultuous than his playing career. After a good first season in charge at Brockville, a breach of discipline by several senior players led to Jim resigning early the following season – a decision Jim regrets and now puts down to inexperience. But it was not quite all over on the playing front. Whilst on a coaching course at Largs, Jim took part in a practice match and his knee held out well. He then spent eight months training and building up his knee, and decided to give playing another go.

The surgeon told me I was off my head, but you're a long time not playing, and I resumed playing with Dundee in 1990, and then moved to Partick Thistle. I wasn't quite the same player. I reckon I had lost 20 or 30 percent off my game. I didn't quite have the same spring, but I learned to read the game better, not having to make as many last-ditch tackles.

What Jim does not dwell on is the pain in his knee after every match he played after his injury – some 200 in all. All he will say is, 'I played on until I was 36. I played in a League Cup Final, won promotion with Partick Thistle and had a couple of seasons back in the Premier League – so not too bad. I've got a sore knee – so what?'

After two seasons at Partick, Jim rejoined Dundee, playing once more in the Premier League for two seasons. Jim took over as player-manager in 1993, but the club were relegated. Jim left the club in 1996 after failing to regain Premier League status. Jim then took over at Hibernian from where he was sacked in 1997.

A two and a half year spell as Chelsea youth coach, where he helped nurture the young John Terry, was followed by a spell as Portsmouth assistant. Jim also coached abroad, but by 2002 he felt ready to return to Scotland. Once more Dundee came calling and he was given the task of picking up the pieces left following the departure of Ivano Bonetti. He now occupies one of the hardest jobs in football, that of Dundee manager, with all the financial restrictions that go with it. How he has coped with the circumstances at Dens Park and the stranglehold around the club has earned the respect of everyone in the game. His many qualities as a player – the do-or-die spirit, 100 percent effort and total commitment to the job in hand – are every bit as evident now as they were when he first entered the game. The very qualities that endeared him to Morton fans have sustained him throughout his career during which he has had many trials and tribulations.

Morton in 1983. Jim Duffy is in the middle row, third from left.

I don't think you would get the same satisfaction from an easy job. In my first season back we finished top six and qualified for Europe. Shortly afterwards we were in administration. Then we reached the Cup Final. When I started out I couldn't have envisaged everything that's happened, but I have no regrets. There's no point in looking back and thinking 'if only'.

In a career full of highs and lows, Dundee's relegation from the Scottish Premier League (SPL) in 2005 ranks as one of Jim's bitterest disappointments. There is no doubt that the situation that Jim inherited at Dens Park when he took over from Ivano Bonetti contributed to Dundee's demise in season 2004–05.

There is no doubt in my mind that the influx of foreign players in the Scottish game has been to the overall detriment of young Scottish players. There have obviously been some outstanding successes, such as Larsson and Laudrup and others, but the cream has been spread quite thin, and over the piece I think more harm than good has been done.

Long-term development has been stunted for a short-term fix. To a degree, I can understand it. Celtic and Rangers, for example, must win every week and they must respond to the demands of the fans. But the bigger clubs must be encouraged to develop their own talent.

The SPL initially had a rule whereby each club had to include two under-21 players in the squad for games, and managers would put young boys on the bench just to justify the criteria, with little or no intention of using them. That's been done away with, but we should have a gradual increase in the number of Scottish players in the squad, so that we eventually have five or six in the squad and being used. That would still leave scope for good foreign players and allow our players to mix with them, and learn their good habits, and hopefully push themselves more. Our international team has suffered accordingly because we don't have enough quality players playing at the highest level.

Jim is in no doubt as to the task that confronts him as Dundee manager. 'I have to pick the club up, and get them promoted in one season, otherwise I'm out of a job. The future for Dundee must be investment in young players, along with good experienced pros to bring them along.'

Morton fans should not get too precious about the depth of feeling between Jim Duffy and Dundee. After all, he is not the first footballer to have made his name at Morton and then moved on to bigger things at Dundee. He was only really retracing Billy Steel's footprints, but such is the impact that Jim made in his three-year spell at Morton that there will forever be a part of Jim Duffy that wears the blue and white hoops.

Morton playing statistics: (League, League Cup, Scottish Cup)

Season	Appearances	Goals
1981–82	20	0
1982–83	34	0
1983–84	49	2
1984–85	37	1

Postscript

As things transpired, Jim was correct in his assertion that his job at Dundee was on the line, although he was never given the chance to return Dundee to the Premier League. Jim was sacked in August 2005 after just three League matches. The team were top of the League, but a Cup defeat against Stranraer sealed his fate. As ever, Jim took the blow on the chin, and will no doubt bounce back into football in some capacity. A football man through and through, it is hard to imagine him not involved in the game that has been his life for 30 years. He may well get the chance to display that legendary Cappielow grit once more.

Chapter 9

Janne Lindberg
A Consummate
Professional

It is a measure of the impression that Janne Lindberg made on Morton Football Club in his two-and-a-half-year spell at Morton that, almost a decade since he left the club, his name is still spoken of in reverential tones. Janne's arrival at Cappielow was a pivotal moment in the recent history of Morton. When Janne arrived at Cappielow in October 1994 with his fellow Finn, Marko Rajamaki, it was to a Morton side playing in the Second Division, the first time the club had sunk so low in 35 years. Manager Allan McGraw was determined to get the club back to the First Division in one season and knew that he needed an injection of class. With Janne Lindberg that is just what he got. Seasoned professionals like Derek Collins and Rowan Alexander acknowledge that it was Janne's influence and drive (not forgetting Marko's flair and goals) that propelled the club back to the First Division and almost to the Premier League in successive seasons. In a recent poll, Janne was voted the eighth greatest Morton player of all time, which says it all about the impact that he made in his all-too-brief career in a Morton jersey.

Janne Lindberg was born in 1966 in the town of Kuusankoski, an industrial town in southern Finland some 80 miles from Helsinki. Like all the Scandinavian

Janne Lindberg.

countries, Finland recognises the importance of starting football skills at a young age and Janne began playing football at the age of six with a club from his home town called Ku Mu. He graduated through the various age groups to the first team. The club yo-yoed between the Finnish first and second divisions and Janne stayed with them until 1990. Janne credits his early development to his father.

My dad was the biggest influence on my career. In the 1970s, football wasn't really a huge part of Finland's culture. There wasn't a lot of money and the teams were mostly part-time. There was some coaching: some good, some not so good. So basically I learned to play by watching my dad and then practising with him. He combined playing with his work and I would follow him around when he played.

Janne then moved to Haka, one of the top sides in Finland, for a year before moving to My Pa 47 in 1992 where he really began to make his name. Janne made his international debut in 1992, the first of 34 caps. My Pa, full name Myllykoski Pallo-47 of Ry, hail from the small town of Anjalankoski not far from Janne's birthplace, and is based in the district of Myllykoski. My Pa are famous as the club who produced Finland's greatest player, Jari Litmanen. Their achievements in recent years are very impressive for a club of their size. Janne won the Finnish Cup with them in 1992, the year they first entered Europe, and in 1995 they knocked Motherwell out of the UEFA Cup. They have continued their rise and are now one of the top clubs in Finland. In Janne's time with the club they were just beginning to build their reputation as one of the top clubs in Finland and Janne gained good experience in European football with them. In all, he spent 11 seasons in the Finnish League, playing 250 matches and scoring 21 goals. He combined his football with working in the town's paper mill; paper manufacturing being the district's main source of economy.

In 1994, Allan McGraw was given a tip-off by Jimmy Pearson, an ex-Morton footballer who had travelled extensively as a coach and at that time was coaching in Finland. Pearson told Allan that two Finnish players were available for transfer to a Scottish club. One was Janne, who Pearson thought extremely highly of, and the other was Marko Rajamaki, Janne's teammate at My Pa. Janne had played against

Janne in action on the pitch against Stirling.

Scotland in September and Allan McGraw went as far as to telephone Scotland coach Craig Brown for his opinion. Brown was fulsome in his praise for Janne and the decision was taken to bring the pair over to Greenock for a three-week trial. Janne remembers being asked if he would like to play in Scotland.

The My Pa manager, Hari Kampman, asked me one day if I would be interested in going to Scotland to play. At that time there were not many Finns playing abroad. It was a surprise and I thought about it and after talking it over with my wife decided to give it a try. I knew all about Scottish football's history and culture. I saw it as a chance to improve my game. Of course it helped that Marko was going as well.

Both players made their debut on 22 October against Berwick Rangers. At this stage of the season, with the first quarter of the programme complete, Morton were in a lowly sixth place, six points behind the leaders Stirling Albion and Berwick Rangers. The gap became eight when Morton lost the match to Berwick 2–1, with Warren Hawke scoring both goals. Allan McGraw had warned the duo about the pace of the Scottish game, and Marko and Janne did find a noticeable difference. Marko, however, impressed with his fast and direct running and Janne displayed a neat touch on the ball, bite in the tackle and a determined attitude, all of which would become the Lindberg trademarks.

The Berwick defeat was Morton's third loss in a row, but McGraw was confident that the Finnish duo could help turn things around. The final two matches of the trial period resulted in the two starring in two home victories for 'Ton and McGraw was of no doubt that he had to keep Marko and Janne. As the trial period drew to a close Janne was reported as saying, 'We would like to stay, although it is not up to us. Everyone at Cappielow has been very friendly and we have had a tremendous reception from the supporters. In Scotland the crowds shout more and the football is faster.' When Janne was asked if he understood the shouts of his new Morton teammates he replied with a smile, 'Perhaps it's better if we don't understand everything!'

Craig Brown, speaking at a dinner in Greenock during this period, warned that Morton would have to be lively if they wanted to keep Janne. He advised the club to snap Janne up before others pinched him from under their noses, and warned that Bolton manager Bruch Rioch had been primed by Mixu Pataleinan, and was ready to swoop. Brown said, 'Janne Lindberg is a brilliant player and if Morton have an opportunity to sign him, they should.'

There was then a period of uncertainty as the then Morton Chairman, John Wilson, stalled and the deal looked dead. Morton director Douglas Rae, however, would not let the matter die and along with Allan McGraw prevailed upon John Wilson to think again.

A fee of £250,000, a considerable outlay for a club like Morton, secured the services of the two Finns. It proved to be money well spent. John Wilson had come in for much criticism from Morton fans for not releasing funds for players. He had a long-stated belief that Morton should never threaten their very existence by spending indiscriminately. His astute stewardship had ensured that Morton were financially viable, but unfortunately it backfired when after a bad run of injuries the club were relegated to the Second Division in 1994. The signing of Lindberg and Rajamaki showed that the club was determined to arrest the slump. It was a significant turning point in Morton's fortunes.

In Janne they had signed a top-quality international with 11 seasons experience in the Finnish League. Marko Rajamaki was in fact born in Gothenburg, Sweden, of Finnish parents. They came as a package. Marko was quite obviously the more flamboyant of the duo, with his long flowing hair and exciting style of play. He scored goals and excited the fans, but it was Janne who firmly established himself as a players' player.

The two Finns officially joined Morton on 11 November when Morton were five points behind the leaders. Janne scored his first 'Ton goal a day later, a 20-yard drive against Brechin in a 3–1 victory. The Morton fans celebrated by unfurling a Finnish flag. Before long, they had adopted the full Viking persona, complete with horned helmets. One churlish critic of this sartorial splendour pointed out that there were not any Vikings from Finland – geography has never been Morton fans' strong point! The arrival of the Finns quite naturally brought back memories of the halcyon days of the 1960s and the first 'Scandinavian Invasion' of the Danish variety.

Janne Lindberg against Stirling.

The signing of the duo had an immediate and dramatic effect on the rest of the Morton side. After one particular match soon after they had signed, a rejuvenated Rowan Alexander told the assembled press, 'I've waited years for this sort of service.'

Janne's work rate, tackling and covering added a new dimension to the side and gave others the confidence to try things that they may otherwise not have tried. Within a month it was obvious that Derek McInnes for one was blossoming beside Janne in midfield. McInnes had just recovered fitness after being sidelined for months with a cruciate injury and was given a great confidence booster when McGraw installed him as captain. Playing alongside Janne gave McInnes the freedom to indulge his undoubted talents. Inspired by Marko and Janne, the side hit a good run of form and topped the table for the first time that season in late February. There were several teams in the race for promotion including Berwick,

Dumbarton and Stirling Albion. Three drawn matches in a row then left 'Ton four points behind leaders Dumbarton with six matches left.

One of the most exciting days of the season was in late April when Dumbarton dropped a point at home and Morton came from 2–0 and 3–2 down away to Berwick to win 4–3. In retrospect it was probably the single most significant result of the season. Berwick were 2–0 up after 12 minutes with another double by Warren Hawke before Morton pulled it back to 2–2. Hawke completed his hat-trick to make the score 3–2 to Berwick. With six sides left in the promotion shake-up, defeat in this match was unthinkable as it could have ruined Morton's promotion hopes. Through it all, Janne remained a composed figure. His cool head and intelligent promptings ensured that Morton came back into the match. Derek Collins equalised and Marko Rajamaki claimed the winner with two minutes left. Marko was beginning to form the happy knack of scoring important late goals – a late equaliser early in the season saving defeat against Brechin. Janne's outstanding performance against Berwick was all the more remarkable as he had played a mid-week international for Finland against the Faroe Islands when not fully fit.

Morton had claimed he was not fit to play, but the Finnish FA had insisted. Janne showed no ill effects and was then instrumental in Morton's rise to the top of the table in the coming weeks. The promotion fight was played out against the background of a series of international matches. Several times during the season Janne and Marko would join up with the Finnish squad, play the international in mid-week and then return to Greenock in time for the club's next match. The situation required a steady hand from Allan McGraw and with two matches left the top of the table looked as follows.

	Played	Points	Goal Difference
Morton	34	58	+19
Dumbarton	34	57	+22
Stirling Albion	34	55	+11

Morton's penultimate match was against Dumbarton at Cappielow in a virtual title decider. Victory for Morton would guarantee promotion and almost certainly the championship. At the end of the 90 minutes a Jimmy Cowan style wonder save from David Wylie, a penalty won by Rajamaki and converted by Derek Lilley, and a 35-yard lob straight out of the Andy Ritchie handbook from Marko won the match and promotion for Morton. After the match, a gutted Dumbarton manager Murdo McLeod described Wylie's save, an instinctive point-blank effort, as the best he had ever seen. A modest Wylie commented, 'You've heard of a Gordon Banks save, well that was a David Wylie save!'

With all the hype surrounding the two Finns and the scoring exploits of Derek Lilley, the contribution of Wylie should not be overlooked. A goalkeeper with excellent reflexes, Wylie was with Morton for 14 seasons, eventually breaking Jim Holmes's appearance record. His total of 542 matches leaves him second in the all-time list behind Derek Collins. The following week the championship was secured with a 1–0 win over Meadowbank and the £250,000 outlay on the Finns had paid off.

However, Allan McGraw had never seen it as a gamble. He knew he was getting a class act in Janne, a player who could comfortably play in the Premier League, and a goalscorer in Rajamaki. As the celebrations were in full swing Janne himself said, 'Watch me go next season. I've played for the last 18 months without a break and I think I can play much better.'

Derek McInnes climaxed a wonderful recovery by winning two club Player of the Year awards and the PFA Second Division Player of the Year. Derek is in no doubt as to his debt to Janne.

Janne made me a more complete player, both on and off the field. He was the consummate professional, so dedicated to his craft. You couldn't fail to play and train with him and become a better player and a better person. Just watching how he went about his business inspired me when I was trying to regain my fitness after my injury. His influence on the whole club and on myself as an individual was immense.

Derek McInnes undoubtedly deserved all the plaudits he received for his match-winning form, but it was Janne's drive that was a key feature in winning the League. He was not the biggest at five feet seven but he had a powerful frame that enabled

Unfortunately this is as close as Janne got to the Scottish Cup in his time with Morton. He is pictured here with Marko Rajamakie.

him to win tackles against much bigger opponents. He was much more than a ball winner of course. He was a creative and calming influence, and his imposing presence allowed McInnes and Mahood much more time on the ball, allowing their talents to flow. Janne's hopes for the following season were both optimistic and prescient. 'I think the side is good enough to challenge for promotion to the Premier League if the players apply themselves and we keep the side together.'

Janne's prediction was almost borne out. Season 1995–96 was one of the most memorable, exhilarating and ultimately disappointing in the club's long history. Consolidation was not a word in Allan McGraw's vocabulary. He knew he had a side capable of winning promotion.

Before a ball was kicked, Allan reckoned he had the best midfield in the First Division in Lindberg, McInnes and Alan Mahood, another who benefited enormously from Janne's presence beside him. In Derek Collins, Allan had one of the best full-backs in the club's history and Derek Lilley was coming of age as a striker. Money was once more made available by John Wilson and £100,000 persuaded Berwick to part with thorn-in-the-side striker Warren Hawke. The jigsaw seemed complete. Despite McGraw's confidence, there were probably very few others who fancied Morton's chances of promotion. They found themselves in arguably the most competitive First Division in living memory. Both Dundee clubs, Dunfermline and St Johnstone were Premier League clubs in everything but status, and even the most faithful Morton fan could not have predicted that 'Ton would do so well in such company.

Ironically, Morton did not make the best of starts, but a win in September over Dunfermline followed by a 4–1 thrashing of county rivals St Mirren kick-started their campaign. These matches saw the best of Janne and Morton then went on a

Janne watches Alan Mahood in a tussle for the ball in 1995.

The Morton fans played a large part in the promotion year of 1995. Here they celebrate a 2–0 victory over Dumbarton.

run that hoisted them up among the leaders. But just as they were in the ascendancy, as so often in their history, they sold one of their top players – in this case Derek McInnes to Rangers. It need not have been a fatal blow if Derek had been replaced with another midfielder. But Morton soldiered on with the same pool and remarkably kept themselves in the promotion race, neck and neck with the more fancied Dunfermline and Dundee United.

Janne was outstanding in this period, softening the blow of McInnes' departure by virtually doing two men's jobs. Taking over the captaincy of Morton (as well as that of Finland), Janne fully demonstrated his leadership qualities. However, the failure to replace McInnes was compounded in February when 'Ton lost two matches in a row heavily to Dunfermline and Dundee United. In early March 1996 the fatal blow was delivered when Janne caught his studs in the turf and had to be

Morton celebrate their victory over Dumbarton and winning the Second Division championship in 1995. Janne Lindberg is second from right, front row.

carried from the field on a stretcher. He had damaged his knee ligaments and missed the remainder of the season.

Without Janne, Morton fought on and remarkably took the promotion race to the last match of the season, ultimately just failing to make the play-offs. It is conjecture of course, but there seems little doubt that, but for Janne's injury, Morton would have finished second at the very least and qualified for the play-offs. And if they had held on to McInnes, so much more could have been achieved. It is significant that with Janne and Derek in the side, new signing Warren Hawke had been a sensation with an excellent scoring record. With the loss of first McInnes and then Janne, Hawke hit a goals drought and never really recaptured his early scoring form.

Almost inevitably the next season was an anti-climax with Morton found more often in the bottom half of the table than the top. Janne struggled with injury,

Morton in 1996–97. Janne is second from the left, front row.

missing a dozen matches and, after scoring 28 goals in his first two seasons, Rajamaki lost his scoring touch. Gradually, what could have been one of the best sides in Morton's history was broken up. Suddenly the old money problems resurfaced and John Wilson decided he had had enough and sold out to Hugh Scott. The blackest period in the club's history was just around the corner.

My last season was not so happy. The club as a unit were not so solid and there were a few problems. I had injuries but that is just part of the game. But I have only good memories of my time with Morton. Everyone was so good to me and Greenock was a nice town with nice people. My family were very happy. My wife and I still watch videos of our time in Greenock with the children.

The two Finns' contracts ran out and in a period of uncertainty, nothing was forthcoming from the club. Janne was given the chance of a move to Germany and

Janne directing the game.

signed for second division side Saarbrucken. 'I would have been quite happy to sign another contract with Morton but the club held off and held off, and it was only after I signed for Saarbrucken that I received a phone call from the club asking me to stay. But by then it was too late.'

Given the events of the next few years at Cappielow, perhaps it was best that Janne did move on, or his memories of his time at Greenock could have been soured by the shenanigans of Mr Scott. Sadly, the club did not build on the legacy of Janne and Marko and the downward spiral almost ended in the demise of the club. In the meantime, Marko had short spells with Hamilton and Livingston before returning home. He is now coaching in Finland, and still keeps in touch with Janne.

Unfortunately, Janne's family did not settle in Germany and he only stayed a year. He returned to Finland and My Pa and played until 2000. He took up a coaching position with My Pa in 2003 and the club have won the Finnish Cup twice since, most recently in 2005. 'Coaching My Pa has allowed me to see a different side of the game. I am learning something every day. You never know what is around the corner. Someday perhaps I will be a coach at a top club, but for now I am very happy.'

Janne credits Allan McGraw as a major influence.

Allan McGraw is one of the best coaches I have played under: a very decent and intelligent man. He took care of everything and looked after my family. I have much to thank him for. My family settled in well in Scotland and we were fortunate to enjoy the terrific Scottish hospitality. My family had a terrific time; everyone made it so easy to settle in. On the pitch it was a memorable period in my life too. I have lots of great memories of my time with Morton, the highlight of which was being chosen to captain the side. Winning the Second Division was memorable as well and I really enjoyed the Cup matches. The difference between the crowds in Finland from the Scottish crowds was very noticeable. In Finland the fans don't make a lot of noise, whereas in Scotland they are very noisy – they always want more and more. I very much enjoyed the home games because of the atmosphere, with the fans singing and shouting my name.

Allan McGraw considers Janne one of his best signings.

Janne was the ideal professional. He always wanted the ball, used it wisely and could always be relied upon to cover for his teammates. He was an international-class player and for us to get him was a real bonus. He allowed others to play and the whole side looked up to him.

Derek Collins remembers Janne's reliability and consistency. 'Janne was just always there when you needed him. He would give you the option of a nice easy ball when you were in trouble and he never gave the ball away. If someone gave the ball away, he would win it back. A great professional.'

The bare statistics – 88 games and five goals – do scant justice to Janne's influence at Morton. He brought a level of professionalism not seen at Cappielow since the 1960s and the arrival of the Danes. When he joined Morton there was a real danger that they would be just another Second Division club. Janne's influence brought Morton fans to within touching distance of Premier League football once more, and for that he is worth his place in any Morton hall of fame.

Morton playing statistics: (League, League Cup, Scottish Cup)

Season	Appearances	Goals
1994–95	29	1
1995–96	29	2
1996–97	30	2

Chapter 10

Benny Rooney
The Best Ever?

As the heatwave summer of 1976 approached, Morton Football Club was at a low ebb. By and large the 1970s had not been kind to Morton fans. Give or take the odd victory over the Old Firm and the infrequent Texaco Cup matches against the likes of Wolves and Newcastle, the decade had been mostly a constant fight against relegation, and the time-worn saga of the club selling their best players to survive. In 1975 they had failed to finish in the top 10 and so missed out on qualifying for the much-vaunted Premier League. A new manager, Joe Gilroy, came and went and the club narrowly escaped relegation to the Second Division at the end of season 1975–76. The highs of the 1960s were a distant memory and the club needed a new start; someone who could pick the club up by its bootlaces and drive them forward. Enter Benny Rooney.

Benny Rooney was born in 1943 in Cambuslang, the son of Bob Rooney, a professional footballer with several Scottish clubs including Clyde and Falkirk. When Benny was four his dad signed for Leyton Orient and the family moved down south. There then followed a defining time in Benny's life when Bob signed for Workington Town in the English Fourth Division. When Benny's dad was forced to retire through injury he became the side's trainer. Workington's manager at the time was Bill Shankly and, like so many others, a 10-year-old Benny fell under Shanks's spell.

Obviously, with that kind of involvement there was only one thing I wanted to do. With my dad at the club I got involved with the training and from about 10 years old I was training along with the players. My dad was the trainer at Workington for about two to three years, working with Bill Shankly. I can still remember those early days. Shanks used to come around to our house after training and we'd sit in front of the fire just talking football. And with a background like that, I caught the bug, and it was always going to be football for me.

When Benny was 12 the family moved back to Scotland and he attended Our Lady's High in Motherwell, a school renowned as something of a football academy. Billy McNeill was captain of the senior side and the entire half-back line of the under-15 side – Bobby Murdoch, John Cushley and Benny Rooney – signed for Celtic within a short space of time. Benny also played juvenile, but on leaving

Benny Rooney and his father.

school he signed for Cambuslang Rangers who were coached by his father. Within a year he was a Celtic player, signing on a provisional form aged 16. He was soon farmed out to Petershill Juniors, following the accepted practice of the time.

Benny acquitted himself well in the juniors but first-team opportunities at Celtic were limited. In 1962, after consultations with his father, who had by now joined up at Parkhead as physio, Benny decided a move was his best option for first-team football and he moved to Dundee United, managed by Jerry Kerr. He stayed at Tannadice for four years doing reasonably well without fully establishing himself, before moving to St Johnstone. This was when his playing career really took off. Signed by Bobby Brown, soon to become Scotland manager, and blossoming under Willie Ormond, who would also eventually become Scotland manager, Benny spent eight good years at Muirton Park. Moving back to centre-half, he captained the side in the 1969 League Cup Final, losing 1–0 to Celtic. The Final was notable for Jock Stein famously banning Bob Rooney from the dug-out as Stein feared he would

Morton in 1979, with Benny Rooney seated in the middle of the front row, in the tracksuit.

become too emotionally involved, with his son playing for the opposition. Benny also played in Europe during a productive spell under Ormond. When Ormond left, Benny moved on to Partick Thistle and captained the side from midfield to the First Division championship in 1976. Benny was looking forward to his first stab at the Premier League at the age of 33 when Morton made their approach.

I'd just come back from holiday when Hal phoned me up. When I was playing it was always my intention to get into management; I had taken all the coaching courses. When it came though, it was out of the blue; I hadn't applied for any jobs. Hal phoned me up, asked me if I wanted to be player-coach and it just went from there.

Hal Stewart knew the game and had many contacts, and it was well known in the game that Benny was a leader and organiser on the field. It would be a natural progression to management and, as Chairman of the Players' Union, Benny was not short of an opinion or two.

Over the years I had worked with quite a number of managers and learned something from all of them – good and bad. Davie McParland signed me for Thistle and he was good for me, as was wee Bertie [Auld] who took over from Davie. But the biggest influence on me was Willie Ormond. He built St Johnstone up into a really good, attractive side and I had my best years as a player there.

Initially, Benny came as player-coach and played in the first six League Cup sectional matches, but as he admits himself, combining the two roles was difficult.

I quickly realised that, being the type of player I was – always having to be involved, organising, etc – that I couldn't give everything to both jobs. I realised that I would have to concentrate solely on the management and training side of things. So I played the length of the League Cup section and then gave the playing side up.

It was sticky at first. There was a lot of reorganising to be done, and I had to wheel and deal a bit, and that was where I learned so much from Hal Stewart. We struck up a good relationship from the start and worked together well. I learned so much from him in the transfer market. There was a bit of clearing out to do and I brought some new faces in, but the nucleus of a good side was there. Mark McGhee was there in the reserves, although he was still a young boy. I switched him to centre-forward, his best position, and he was a revelation. The big thing though was to get the players fit. We changed the training to three nights a week and really worked them hard. We got them fit and strong, and working together. I was lucky in that there was some good kids there like Neil Orr and John McNeil – thanks to Ronnie Ahlfield who had done a great job on the youth side of things. And Allan McGraw was a great help to me in the early days.

When I took over it was only myself, Allan, Ronnie and Willie Gray the kit man. Allan had been taking the reserves and then helped me with the first team. He then had to go into hospital for an operation and that was a loss, but he came back and was running the reserves the year we won promotion. The reserves won their league as well the same year, which was amazing, thanks to Allan.

Within a very short space of time Allan McGraw's reserve side provided several players for the first team and, as Allan recalls, the transformation from reserve football to first-team action was very smooth. 'Benny liked the reserves to play in the same way as the first team, so that they could step straight in, without any undue disruption.'

For Benny the progression from giving up the playing side to concentrating solely on management was a smooth transition. 'I know most players when they give up to move into management say that they miss playing. But I never did. I just got so involved with the management thing. I had found my niche and I loved it.'

Benny knew he had a tough task ahead of him. The club had stagnated and needed someone with the drive and ambition to elevate the club to greater heights. It was not all doom and gloom though. He had inherited some talented players. Roy Baines was one of the best goalkeepers in the country. Davie Hayes and George Anderson were only 22, but had been regulars in the first team for six seasons. There were good pros like John Goldthorpe and Jim Townsend, and 17-year-olds

John McNeil and Neil Orr were on the fringes of the first team. There was also the teenage Mark McGhee, bursting with natural ability, but frustrated at lack of first-team action.

I had been a youth-team player with Bristol City and then shortly after I joined Morton the manager Erik Sorensen left and Joe Gilroy took over. He was only there a season and I didn't have too much contact with him, so Benny was really the first guy to put his arm around me and actually talk to me. He gave me great encouragement and made me focus on my game. I was probably a frustrating player to manage at the time because I would run with the ball and lose it. Benny showed me how to use other options. He also gave me a lot of sound advice that probably didn't mean much at the time, but later on at Aberdeen I realised that Fergie was telling me the same thing. I also thought he was very laid back; nothing seemed to faze him.

As Benny says, he quickly retired after the League Cup sectional matches. A 7–1 drubbing of Cowdenbeath perhaps gave false hope, as they lost the last sectional match and failed to qualify for the quarter-finals, starkly bringing to the fore the realities of the task Benny faced. He switched Jim Holmes from midfield to left-back and began moulding his team. Initially it was one step forward and two back until, in October 1976, Benny managed to secure the signing of Andy Ritchie from Celtic.

We signed Andy through the goalkeeping situation. Celtic wanted Roy Baines and I knew all about Andy. I knew what I was taking on, but I knew what he could give us. Roy was a good 'keeper but I felt I could always replace him. The deal went through without a hitch. Andy came in and just started being Andy, and he quickly gelled with Mark McGhee.

Andy was an immediate hit with the Morton fans with his sensational skills and memorable goals, although it took a while for the Scottish press to catch on. By the first few months of 1977, the team that Benny built was beginning to be noticed, thanks to a terrific undefeated run consisting of the last 16 League matches. They eventually finished a creditable fourth as St Mirren ran away with the League, but the ever astute Bob Crampsey observed that Morton just might be the team to watch the following season in a First Division that included full-time Hearts and Dundee. And so it proved. With virtually the same side, Morton picked up the 1977–78 season where they had left off, remaining undefeated in their first 11 matches before falling at home to a Queen of the South side managed by Mike Jackson, who would soon have a big influence on Morton's future.

That defeat ended the club's record of 27 matches (22 wins and five draws) unbeaten, but Benny had learned much from it. He knew the midfield lacked a ball-winning, energetic player. He filled the gap with some short-term signings but had to wait until March before he secured Greenock-born Jimmy Miller's signature from Motherwell for a bargain £10,000. Benny had identified a weakness in the midfield and knew that the all-action Miller could fill it. Miller formed a formidable partnership with the unsung Tommy Veitch, who had arrived for pennies via Hartlepool and Halifax. Veitch played a largely unnoticed but vital role in the promotion season.

But before Benny could sign Miller he had to lose a star player. By Christmas 1977, Morton had forged ahead in the League, with the brilliant Ritchie as orchestral leader, feeding the hungry and eager Mark McGhee. Mark McGhee had scored 16 goals in 20 League matches and was a wanted man. He was transferred to Newcastle for £150,000 just before the New Year. It was a blow to Benny to lose the exciting, emerging talent of McGhee and an early lesson on the harsh realities of managing a club like Morton. He now had to regroup his side and find a replacement for McGhee, as the cynics wrote Morton off – not for the first or last time.

Benny did not replace McGhee until March. He was prepared to wait until the right player became available at the right price. The signing of the small but rumbustious striker Bobby Russell from Alloa Athletic – for yet another bargain fee of £10,000 – proved to be the trump card. Russell scored eight goals in the final 10 League matches – a vital statistic given that 'Ton eventually won the League on goal difference.

St Johnstone captain Benny with Real Madrid captain Gento in 1970.

I actually signed Bobby Russell without having seen him play. He was recommended by a newspaper reporter. I had quite a good relationship with some of the reporters who covered the lower division matches and we were tipped off about Bobby Russell. So I sent Ronnie Ahlfield to watch him just the once, and he came back raving about him, and I signed him up for £10,000.

The 1977–78 season for Morton was characterised by a number of postponed matches and from about February, Morton were always trailing behind rivals Dundee and Hearts in terms of matches played. As a consequence, after leading for much of the season, by the third week in March, Morton were four points behind Dundee and two behind Hearts with games in hand. With the addition of Miller and Russell, Benny now had a settled side and systematically began to erode the gap. With two matches left to play they were again top and a win over Airdrie at Cappielow in front of 8,000 fans memorably sealed promotion and, as it turned out, the championship. Benny believes that the long unbeaten run of 27 matches was the key to success.

We didn't begin the season with any great hopes of promotion. Hal had basically brought me in initially to sort things out, but as the run went on and on, and we were at the top for so long, we realised it was there for us, and we wanted it. At the start I wasn't thinking of promotion, but as things progressed so quickly, we saw it there in front of us, especially after the undefeated run we had. After Queen of the South beat us, we buckled down and picked it up again. We knitted together again. The players that had been there a while, really good players like Charlie Brown, Davie Hayes and George Anderson, drove us on.

Benny had delivered Premier League football inside two years. Progress had been quick and dramatic – and for a profit. Of the £150,000 McGhee transfer fee, only around £20,000 had been spent on bringing players in. Benny had signed Jim Holmes, Tommy Veitch and Barry Evans for nothing. For the assault on the Premier League it was obvious that some more money had to be spent. Benny signed three players – Ally Scott, Jim Rooney and Bobby Thomson – for a combined sum of only

Benny relaxes in a
rare quiet moment.

£30,000. Ally Scott was signed on a free transfer after unsuccessful spells with Hibs and Rangers. Jim Rooney was signed from Queens Park, so there was no transfer fee involved, and Benny paid the largest transfer fee in all his time at Cappielow for Thomson who he knew from their St Johnstone days. One of his most important signings was on the non-playing side when Mike Jackson joined as Benny's assistant, and the two bonded immediately.

Mike was great for me and the club. It was a great partnership. We got ourselves in trouble at times, but we rallied round. I also had great help from Gordon Whitelaw and Barney Jensen. Again the key for us for the first season in the Premier was to get the players as fit as possible and to sign runners. That was why I signed Ally Scott. Not the greatest of footballers perhaps, but a great chaser of lost causes. He was an ideal player who, if we were under pressure, we could hit the ball into corners and he would chase it. Jim Rooney was very fit, a real dynamo who would run all day, but could play a bit as well. But big Bobby [Thomson] was the one we really wanted and he was great for us for a couple of seasons, despite his faults.

Morton lost their first three Premier matches, but Benny refused to panic, sensing that things would turn around. A victory against Dundee United at Tannadice in the fourth match was the turning point, and gave the team the confidence and impetus to move forward. With Ritchie in sensational form, and more good young players in the shape of Joe McLaughlin and Jim Tolmie beginning to emerge, the future was bright, and Morton comfortably retained their Premier status. Roy Baines had returned from Celtic, giving the defence a more secure and confident look, and although Benny did not have a huge pool of players at his disposal, competition for places was keen.

Even Benny could not have envisaged how well Morton would do for the first half of season 1979–80. Bobby Thomson was in outstanding form, John McNeil was finding some consistency to match his undoubted talents, and Ritchie was still scoring and making the most breathtaking goals. Before long Rooney's exciting side swept to the top of the Premier League. 'You start to think "My God, we're doing it here!" and I would get exasperated when I would ask to bring players in and the board would say that they couldn't afford it, although in fairness they set me a budget and I had to work within it.'

Rarely out of the top three from the first match of the League programme, Morton topped the Premier League for the first time in early November 1979. A 0–0 draw at home to St Mirren, with a missed penalty by Ritchie, was looked upon as a point dropped, but Celtic lost to Kilmarnock and Morton were top on goal difference. After 12 matches they had scored 28 goals. The following week they travelled north and defeated Aberdeen 2–1 to confirm their credentials as live contenders for major honours. In early December they were second, but only on goal difference. There seemed no stopping them as they reached the League Cup semi-final against Aberdeen at Hampden during this memorable spell. Aberdeen were a side that Benny Rooney's Morton could seemingly beat at will, yet in the game that mattered most against them, they froze somewhat and lost the match 2–1. 'In a sense, it was our first big game, the first at Hampden and we didn't do ourselves justice, but we did have a goal chalked off for a ridiculous offside decision that would have levelled the match.'

Undeterred, Morton approached the new decade neck and neck with Celtic at the top of the League, and ironically went top again on goal difference after the semi-final as Celtic had lost a League game on the same day. This was the same Saturday that over 20,000 fans turned up at Easter Road to watch George Best play for Hibs against Partick Thistle. Within a few weeks, two controversial matches against both Old Firm clubs would derail Morton's season and leave a bitter taste for years to come. The Morton versus Rangers match at Cappielow one week after the Aberdeen semi-final has entered the folklore of Scottish football thanks to the infamous Bobby Thomson and Sandy Jardine 'cheat' incident when Thomson was sent off for allegedly butting Jardine. Benny diplomatically remembers the incident. 'There's no way Thomson touched Jardine. But the referee obviously thought he did and sent him off.'

Two weeks later Morton lost 3–1 to Celtic at Parkhead and had Jim Holmes sent off for claiming that Celtic's second and decisive goal should have been disallowed when Dom Sullivan left the field of play and then re-entered to square the ball for to score. So, a season that had promised so much finished in disappointment.

Benny Rooney with Hal Stewart in 1978.

Morton eventually finished sixth in the League, an improvement of one place from the previous season. In retrospect it was still a tremendous achievement for a part-time club.

The team that Benny built had one last hurrah – a Scottish Cup semi-final against Rangers in 1981. Once more the match ended in some controversy as Morton allowed themselves to get involved in a kicking match and had two players sent off in a 2–1 defeat.

There had been a lot of hype before the game about it being a physical match and in the event that's how it turned out. In hindsight you could say I should have played big Andy from the start. [Fearing a physical match, Benny controversially left star man Andy Ritchie on the bench.] We got too involved in the physical stuff and, after letting a lot go in the first half, the referee came down heavy on us in the second half. But looking back on it now, a few of our players did lose the head a bit and that's what cost us the game.

After the Rangers defeat the team began to break up as Benny lost his best players in big money transfers. Orr, Tolmie and Thomson all left in a short space of time and the remainder of Benny's time at Cappielow was spent battling relegation.

We weren't bringing in any money, the board just didn't generate any cash at all; they just sat back. At the finish up the only way we made any money was by selling players. That's when we had fall-outs, nothing major, but it did become frustrating. We were looking to strengthen the team but were constantly losing good players and replacing them with ones who just weren't up to the required standard, apart of course from Jim Duffy. The board's answer to everything was to sell. In terms of going full-time, it would have given us more time with the players to work on things. It wouldn't have helped fitness-wise; we were as fit as anyone. But if we had been full-time it would have helped preparation-wise. We wouldn't have had to bring the guys in on the Saturday morning when we worked on what we were going to do in the matches. In training we had to let technique fall by the wayside because for me fitness was the key. At the time [late 1970s] Dundee United were of the same status as us with the same average crowds. They kept their best players and were able to progress.

Benny's point is well made. In the season that Morton lost to Aberdeen in the League Cup semi-final, Dundee United went on to beat the Dons in the Final for their first major trophy. In the season that Morton were relegated, United won the League and by the following season they were European Cup semi-finalists. Benny and Mike could not constantly deliver with one hand behind their backs and in 1982–83, Morton finished second bottom of the League and were relegated. Benny and Mike Jackson had no inkling as to what would happen next.

The situation by then had become very frustrating, but I never envisaged being sacked, although the club said I wasn't sacked. I arrived for what I thought was a normal board meeting and I had prepared a presentation showing how I was going to make cuts with the definite aim of bouncing back to the Premier League in one season. Before I had the chance to say anything the Chairman, Hugh Currie, started to read from a prepared statement. The words 'We'll have to let Mike Jackson go' jumped out at me. I protested, telling them there was no need for that if they would listen to what I had to say. And he then said that they couldn't afford to keep me either and were letting me go. The word 'sack' was never used but that's what it amounted to. I was prepared to take a wage cut and if they had broached the subject in a different manner that's what would have happened. The reason they gave me was that we were getting paid too much for the job that we were doing. It wasn't for getting relegated. The most disappointing thing was that I classed these men as friends, family friends, and there had been no hint of what they had in mind.

For Mike Jackson, the sacking was a dagger in the heart. 'It was the worst moment of my career. Although you learn to expect anything in football, I really didn't see it coming, and I don't think it was down to cost-cutting, which is what the board said at the time.'

Benny is presented with a plaque commemorating the 27-match unbeaten run in 1977.

Mike took Morton to a tribunal and won his case. Benny had only 11 months left on his contract which was soon settled, so would it not have made sense to keep him at least until his contract expired? The directors claimed that the club was losing more than £4,000 a week and that drastic measures had to be taken or the club would go bust. The official line from Morton was that it was a cost-cutting exercise, but they eventually ended up with another management duo in Tommy McLean and Tom Forsyth, who would not have come cheaply. The suspicion lurks that there was a hidden agenda or that Benny and Mike were scapegoats paying the price for the board selling their best players and failing to replace them. The board just did not share Benny and Mike's vision and could not keep pace with their ambitions. The Morton directors sadly took the route open to people who are involved in football but do not really understand it, and got rid of the most visible asset. Two years earlier, Benny had turned down the chance to take over the vacant Partick Thistle job, but he had found that loyalty counted for very little in football. 'Well, we fell out with Hal over it, but a few months later we were friends again. But looking back after the great times we had, it was sad. It was shattering at the time, but you get on with it.'

The Morton fans greeted the news of Benny's sacking with anger and bemusement and the *Greenock Telegraph* was of the opinion that 'The decision to sack a man that Morton cannot afford to lose is remarkable and astonishing.'

Apologists for the board's decision may point out that Morton won promotion back to the Premier League in one season, but they then spent a yo-yo existence between the Leagues, which again must be put down to their unwillingness to generate adequate finances. From 1983, when Benny left the club, to Jim McInally's appointment 21 years later, Morton have had no less than 14 managers and that includes Allan McGraw's 12-year tenure. Truly, Morton fans never had it so good as under Benny Rooney. Allan McGraw has no doubts as to Benny's place in Morton's history.

Benny will go down as one of the great Morton managers. He sorted the whole club out and changed it for the better. The side that he built was a hard team to handle, full of individual characters, but he gelled them together. I don't know how he handled them at times, but he did it brilliantly. I think basically he got the best out of them by getting them to work hard for one another. He was a great bloke to work for and it was football's loss when he quit the game.

Benny himself acknowledges that a lot of what he achieved could not have been possible without his assistant Mike Jackson. 'Mike was and is a complete football enthusiast. He talks football all the time, thinks football all the time and he played a big part in our success. We're still close now and talk nearly every day.'

Nowadays, Mike looks back on his time at Morton with great pleasure.

I had a fabulous seven years at Celtic and a great time at Queen of the South, but the five years I spent at Morton were the best five years of my football career. What we achieved as a part-time club was unbelievable. Think about it. It was a 10-club Premier League with two going down. Rangers and Celtic were never going to be relegated. Add to that the fact that Aberdeen and Dundee United had their best sides ever, and you're left with two out of six going down. So, for us to survive for so long, play so well for so long and finish so high in the League so often was a fantastic achievement.

Every day was an exciting challenge. I used to love going to Parkhead and Ibrox

and plan out how we were going to approach the game. Every season was an adventure. We would look over the fixture list at the start of the season and plan it out. A point here, two points there. The players deserve enormous credit. The tragedy was that the directors couldn't see it the same as us. If we had gone full-time we might have been able to attract a better class of player. Benny had a great desire to win

Benny with Hal Stewart.

and all he asked was that the players gave of their best, worked hard and were as fit as possible.

It's a bit of a myth that it was our Celtic connection that brought us together. We were at Celtic at the same time, but I'm four years older than Benny. It was actually through a mutual friend, Billy McNeill, that we got together. Benny was a good man-manager and very tactically aware. Against the likes of Aberdeen he would just put wee Danny Docherty on Strachan and we did very well against them to say the least. We gelled immediately. When he asked me to come to Morton, I told him I wasn't going as a yes man, and I was allowed my say, but he made the final decision. I always told him that if and when it all went pear-shaped it would be him they would come after and not me. Shows you how much I knew!

Benny was soon back in management, taking over for a few months at Albion Rovers, where he had a short-lived reunion with Andy Ritchie. In 1984 he was again offered the Partick manager's job and this time accepted. But he soon found that the restrictions on him were even more onerous than in his latter days at Morton. 'Thistle had just been relegated and they expected to bounce back to the Premier in one season. But they had no money and were in a mess. Needless to say we didn't go up and that was me for that job.'

Benny's next job was with the club where he began his career – Celtic. Benny enjoyed a rewarding five-year spell in charge of youth development at Parkhead working with Bobby Lennox. He lost that job during Liam Brady's tenure at the club, when he was sacked by the Irishman who was finding the job too much for him.

Sadly for Benny, that was the final straw. He had again lost a job that he loved and basically he had had enough. Benny has never worked in football since. He entered the licensed trade in the early 1990s and now has his own pub in Glasgow's south side. The general consensus among football people is that Benny was lost to the game too soon, a feeling that Benny himself agrees with.

I feel I had so much more to offer. I had a few offers after I left Celtic, but it would

Benny Rooney with managing director Hal Stewart in 1978, celebrating Morton's promotion to the Premier Division.

Benny Rooney shares the dressing room celebrations with captain Davie Hayes, chairman Hugh Currie and Hal Stewart.

have taken a really big offer to bring me back. It frustrates me a wee bit now when I see how certain teams play and the lack of basic fitness. I'm not bitter about what happened to me. I just get a wee bit angry when I look back on it. But you have to get on with life and look after your family. The time I miss it is when I get together with football people. When I look back at some of the players we had at Morton. Andy Ritchie – Player of the Year. Jim Duffy – Player of the Year. We had McLaughlin and Orr – two Scotland Under-21 centre-backs. I look back on that with a bit of pride and the joy I get from the number of Morton fans who still write to me. That means a lot to me. I've said it time and time again that the best years of my entire career were at Morton.

For many Morton fans Benny Rooney is the best Morton manager ever. That debate will rage on, but what cannot be denied is the fact that Benny Rooney put Morton Football Club on the map and gave the club a standing in Scottish football that they may never achieve again – at least for the foreseeable future. He also signed some of the best players seen at the club since the 1940s and was responsible for some great football and great memories. If nothing else Benny should be thanked for nurturing hopes and dreams and providing one of the finest sides ever seen at Cappielow. That is Benny Rooney's great achievement.